D1270860

© JUDI PARKS

HOUSTON
CITY IN MOTION

ROMEO/ YIAN C- LANGIT

© JIM OLIVE / STOCKYARD PHOTOS

H O U S
C I T Y

I N T R O D U C T I O N   B Y
N E L L I E   C O N N A L L Y

T O N

IN MOTION

URBAN
TAPESTRY
SERIES
TOWERY
PUBLISHING, INC

ART DIRECTION BY

ENRIQUE ESPINOSA

© RAY SOTO PHOTOGRAPHY

Contents

AFTER HAVING TRAVELED THE GLOBE—TO MORE THAN 70 countries and many great cities—Houston remains one of my favorite places. In every city, I have found something special to enjoy. But Houston is the one city that has it all! It is a great, thriving place to work and live, with its many businesses, fine hotels, wonderful restaurants, international flavor, the world-renowned Texas Medical Center, and so much more.

When John and I left the Governor's Mansion in Austin, we made our home on River Oaks Boulevard in Houston. Our family loved living in Houston with its many parks, wonderful theater, ballet, world-class symphony, opera, libraries, fine schools, big city government—everything.

For a very personal reason, I will always have deep affection and gratitude for Houston. I will never forget that at one of the lowest points in my life—when John died—Houston took me into its heart. The people of this community involved me in so many activities that I had little time to dwell on my sadness. I met many fine people whom I remember fondly to this day.

There is a wonderful spirit of volunteerism in Houston. I will always be admiring of this city for what she does for all of us—encouraging us to do what we can for her! She is a great city, constantly in motion—ever changing and growing—becoming more vibrant and alive each year, with open arms to all and a drive for continuous improvement.

I am certain that if you lived and worked and played here, you would love it too!

— **NELLIE CONNALLY**

◆ © JIM OLIVE / STOCKYARD PHOTOS

© RAY SOTO PHOTOGRAPHY

CITY IN MOTION

to alter reality. Whenever nature has reared its head, Houston has taken it by the horns and yanked it into a bit more tolerable form. Born of innovative citizens, necessity, or just plain cussedness, Houston has come to be recognized as a city with the ability to mold and invent itself in all sorts of advantageous ways, making it a mighty interesting place to live or visit.

The most remarked upon example of Houston's style is, perhaps, the Astrodome. When it opened in 1965, the Dome was an instant symbol of Houstonians' thumbing their noses at the heat and humidity that had theretofore combined to make baseball a near-impossible proposition for players and fans alike. No matter how much beer and Big Red soda was iced down, heatstroke had been a real possibility even during night games.

So, air-conditioned baseball and fake grass (dubbed Astroturf, of course) were invented. The whole affair was quickly declared a bona fide Wonder of the World. Not only did the Astrodome pave the way for other (and, wouldn't you know, bigger) domed stadiums in other cities with less-than-congenial climates, but its novelty value alone ensured that it would symbolize Houstonians' ability to tinker with the world—and enhance it where need be.

Nowadays, the Astros make their home at a brand new ballpark downtown, but even this one—Enron Field—has a retractable roof. On the few days when the sky isn't milky from haze and humidity, or when the sun isn't so hot it's curdling the players' sweat, the roof can be rolled back. The team has, in a sense, graduated to even more impressive quarters, once again helping to cut the edge of the future by playing in a state-of-the-art ballpark with a stunning view of the office towers that soar from the asphalt prairies downtown.

While Houston didn't invent air-conditioning, it deserved to. Back in the 1930s, the arrival of air-conditioning transformed the city, often in profound ways. No longer did ⟶

© SCOTT TEVEN PHOTOGRAPHY

◆ © BARRY CHAMPAGNE

© JIM OLIVE / STOCKYARD PHOTOS

CITY IN MOTION

Houstonians have to leave for Galveston or Minnesota during the long, hot summer months. Business activities—in the form of oil, shipping, manufacturing, and commerce—could go on year-round. Houston's debt to air-conditioning goes far beyond the personal comfort factor and becomes a primary determinant in the city's rise as an international business center.

Another example of Houston's bending reality to suit its needs is the Houston Ship Channel. The city had been built along a string of bayous that were too muddy and shallow and full of truly ugly fish to ever qualify as a major port. Forget floating tankers and cargo liners up these winding little streams. So city leaders built the ship channel, which opened in 1914—after more than 50 years of construction—and quickly became the conduit for all manner of crude and refined petroleum products, as well as heavy cargo and agricultural products. Houston, which was previously only a moderate-sized port, was on its way to becoming one of the world's biggest.

Other examples of the city's ability to reinvent itself—and the natural order of things—are boundless. NASA's relentless genius allowed man not only to defy gravity, but to escape Earth's confines altogether and travel to the Moon. The whole thing was coordinated right here at the Johnson Space Center.

A group of heart surgeons (including famed doctors like Michael DeBakey and Denton Cooley) went one step beyond what was thought to be possible and created a whole slew of procedures for revitalizing sick and damaged hearts; today, their once revolutionary processes have become common weapons in the physician's arsenal.

And despite precious few days when the thermometer dips below freezing, the city has the Galleria—year-round ice skating, dining, and shopping under the skylight three stories up. That's just scratching the surface, of course. Beneath the city's surface—literally—there is a growing network of several miles of air-conditioned tunnels that link many of downtown's major buildings. Turning the antisnow strategy employed in northern cities like Toronto on its ear, Houstonians have found these tunnels to be ideal places to set up a shop or grab a cup of coffee during their daytime errands. ⟫

© RAY SOTO PHOTOGRAPHY

◆ © RAY SOTO PHOTOGRAPHY

▼ © WALTER JIMÉNEZ

CITY IN MOTION

No, Houston certainly isn't afraid to monkey with anything from gravity to the weather to baseball to the human heart. The result, almost without exception, is something good—not just for the city, but for the entire world.

Despite this knack for innovation, Houston is a city that has managed to maintain its traditions and its cultural sensibilities as well as any city its size—which is to say, any sprawling, world-class megalopolis. In the shadows of the soaring commercial towers downtown, and throughout the vast suburban areas, are plenty of examples of ways that Houston has come to represent many of the world's finest businesses, art and sports organizations, educational institutions, and recreational outlets.

The city's parks, for instance, are numerous and rewarding. Hermann Park, near downtown, is a fine example of a big city park, with Miller Outdoor Theater offering all sorts of music and drama during the warmer months (unlike most of the city, it's decidedly un-air-conditioned), the Museum of Natural Science offering everything from stars to dinosaurs, and the Houston Zoo offering all manner of interesting animals to go and gawk at. Throughout the city are other fine parks, including the huge Memorial Park, and just about all of them offer plenty of incentive to get out of the car and find out that the city's outdoors is often downright delightful, no matter how hot it may be.

It might seem incongruous in a city known for huge oil companies, a booming commercial sector, and a skyrocketing population, but the values of the frontier are still highly regarded here. People pay homage to the cowboy ethic everywhere from corporate boardrooms to neighborhood gatherings, stressing a straight-up and dead-honest approach to problems large and small. But really, there's little of the Old West here. After all, this is the fourth- or fifth-largest urban area in the country (depending on which population estimate you go by). Modern-day Houston is an international, cosmopolitan city—one with an array of cultural and ethnic influences, a thriving business and commercial sector, and an almost inexhaustible collection of resources for having fun or getting smart. ➤

© WALTER JIMÉNEZ

◆ © JANICE RUBIN

© THOMAS ARLEDGE

CITY IN MOTION

The business community is commonly perceived as floating solely on oil—a perception that's based on plenty of experience. In 1901, oil was discovered in nearby Beaumont, and soon thereafter, it was located by wildcatters throughout the area, along with plenty of natural gas, sulfur, and lime. From the early decades of the 20th century, the city grew in large measure on the fortunes of the increasingly important petrochemical industry. Oil helped fuel (no pun intended) the city's growth into a variety of industrial concerns, and oil helped make Houston the huge and prosperous city that it is. Today, the city is known worldwide as a leader in oil and petrochemical concerns.

But Houston has always had plenty of other resources up its sleeve. Thanks to the ship channel, the city has been a major port for almost as long as it's been an oil mecca. Houston currently hosts the third-largest port in the country, with more than 80 million tons of cargo moving through it each year. Thanks to clear skies and good weather, the city has evolved into a major aerospace R&D center. And thanks to enormous expanses of ranches and farms in the area, Houston is still the hub for a tremendous amount of agricultural activity, with cotton, cattle, and rice all contributing heavily to the city's economic strength.

So, while oil is certainly the dominate component of the economic stew—as evidenced by the various booms and busts that occasionally rattle the city's entire economy—there is plenty more to Houston's business life than most folks (even Houstonians) give it credit for.

You could well say the same thing about the city's arts and cultural organizations. From the highbrow to the highfalutin, Houston's got something going on every weekend, usually at any hour of the day. Museums like the Museum of Fine Arts, the Contemporary Arts Museum, and the Menil Collection offer permanent exhibits and rotating displays of some of the most interesting—and most important—painting and sculpture in the country. Even the lesser-known presentations of art here are often rewarding. To cite just one example, there's a haven of abstract expressionism nestled near downtown, adjacent to the University of St. Thomas campus. There, the Rothko Chapel is a nondenominational sanctum, a special ➠

© BIL OLIVE

◆ © JIM OLIVE / STOCKYARD PHOTOS

© SCOTT HALLERAN / ALLSPORT USA

CITY IN MOTION

place for quiet reflection, with 14 huge canvases by Mark Rothko hanging in splendid silence. Outside the chapel is another work from the same school—Barnett Newman's *Broken Obelisk*, a sculpture that a good many of the city's art aficionados didn't quite "get" at first, and which was hastily relocated to its current home after a debate over its artistic merits. Time has rendered the verdict on both Rothko and Newman, and their world-renowned works now speak for themselves.

It's been said that Texans are people who don't cotton to the performing arts because they can't set them in the corner of their vast living room, prop their boots up on the coffee table, and admire them in the evening. Judging from Houston's performing arts organizations, nothing could be further from the truth. The city has a professional symphony orchestra, professional ballet company, professional opera company, and professional theater—a claim that can be made by only a handful of cities around the world. And fewer cities than that can appreciate the arts in such fine facilities as Jones Hall, the Wortham Theater Center, or the Alley Theater.

To try and run down the numerous venues for singing and dancing and watching and listening to popular music and drama would be impossible. Everything from theaters and galleries at the area's colleges and universities to coffee shops and dance halls is well represented throughout Houston, which offers almost every imaginable folk and pop art form. Indigenous country swing, all manner of Hispanic styles, alternative rock, Celtic, folk, bluegrass, old-time, soul, what have you—in Houston, it's happening somewhere, just about every night.

Sports fans are almost, but not quite, as well accommodated as those who favor the arts. That's not to slight the pro and college teams in town; it's meant to compliment the wide and polished array of arts organizations. Sports are well loved throughout Texas, and Houston is as avid as any city in the state. The Astros often seem to be in the race for a pennant, while the Rockets have two NBA crowns to their credit. And, since the WNBA's inception in 1997, the Houston Comets and Coach Van Chancellor have been the league champions each year. The Oilers moved away a few years back and morphed into the Tennessee Titans, and while ➧

© BRIAN BAHR / ALLSPORT USA

© JIM OLIVE / STOCKYARD PHOTOS

▼ © JIM OLIVE / STOCKYARD PHOTOS

CITY IN MOTION

football is wildly popular in these parts, there has not been what you'd call an outpouring of grief over their departure. Fans content themselves with the realization that pro football is destined to return to Houston sometime soon, and leave it at that.

Meanwhile, they've got plenty to cheer about at local college games, as teams from the University of Houston, Texas Southern University, and Rice University play host to some of the best football in the region. And on the high school level, Houston is—like all of Texas— something akin to manic.

Houston's idea of having a good time is by no means confined to spectator sports. The calendar features something new and big and special just about every month, starting with the Houston Livestock Show and Rodeo (still known by many under its old name, the Fat Stock Show) in February, and continuing through the year with such annual events as the Bayou City Art Festival and Houston International Festival (both in April), the Pin Oak Charity Horse Show in May, the Juneteenth Blues Festival (an event that originated in Texas, but is now widely copied throughout the country), the Jazz Festival in August, the Fiestas Patrias in September, and the holiday celebrations during the cool and rainy spell otherwise known as winter.

But winter, or what passes for it around here, is not the dominant season. Sure, it gets cold enough when a blue norther passes through, but the chill rarely lingers for more than a few days. It's not unusual to see people playing touch football in short sleeves on Christmas, or to go for a swim on St. Patrick's Day.

Maybe, in a roundabout way, Houston's long spells of warm (or even hot) weather have helped to shape the city's character. Not only did the heat hasten the use of air-conditioning, it also has kept Houstonians keenly aware of their surroundings. The flat terrain and the piney woods may not, let's face it, be the most beautiful stretch of real estate in the country, but it's got its merits. Newcomers are often taken aback by the tendency of the streets to flood, or the crawfish in the drainage ditches, or the fire ants that seem to threaten every picnic. ▬➡

© WALTER JIMÉNEZ

◆ © JIM OLIVE / STOCKYARD PHOTOS

© JIM OLIVE / STOCKYARD PHOTOS

CITY IN MOTION

But Houston has not merely coped, it has thrived. Kids hereabouts learn this central fact in their eighth-grade Texas history classes, when they review the city's hardscrabble origins. They learn how the Allen brothers—John and Augustus—bought up a bunch of scrubland along Buffalo Bayou back in 1836 and commenced making nearly outlandish claims about the land's virtues right from the start. Although the city was quickly proclaimed the capital of the new Republic of Texas, the city named for Sam Houston was, in fact, a virtually uninhabitable exercise in real estate speculation, populated mainly by mosquitoes, snakes, and garfish lurking in the spidery network of bayous and creeks that creased the flat landscape. (The legislature lasted here only two years before decamping for more sanguine climes around Austin.)

And yet, armed with a wildly enhanced map of the "city," the Allens and other early entrepreneurs managed to sell investors and pioneers on the notion that this was, indeed, a great port. Houston, they proclaimed with considerable overstatement, was the "great interior commercial emporium of Texas."

Well, although this wasn't exactly true, the nascent Houston spirit determined that it *could* be, and hence that it *must* be. Early residents began the process of bending reality to fit their needs. Mother Nature had dealt them floods and yellow fever; to spite the elements, Houston built, in 1840, a fine dock and began shipping cotton, cattle, mules, and sugar cane from the farms and ranches further inland. When Galveston was wiped out by hurricane and flood in 1900, the city was ready to take its place as the gulf's leading port, and has held onto this role ever since.

And they built the ship channel. And oil was discovered, and the pipelines immediately found their way to the storage and shipping and refining facilities along the ship channel. And baseball was brought indoors. And man walked on the Moon.

And anyone wanting to speculate as to what limits there might be in the future is advised to take stock of all of this, and to bear in mind that Houston is no happy accident. It is, instead, an ongoing exercise in taking the difficult and the fortunate together and molding them into something grand, something exciting, something called home. ●

© JANICE RUBIN

© JIM OLIVE / STOCKYARD PHOTOS

© JIM OLIVE / STOCKYARD PHOTOS

© JIM OLIVE / STOCKYARD PHOTOS

THE HUM OF ACTIVITY ALONG Houston's distinctive skyline reflects the city's steady growth. In fact, through development and acquisition, the Texas hot spot has become the fourth-largest city in the United States.

© JIM OLIVE / STOCKYARD PHOTOS
© JEFF GREENBERG / PHOTOPHILE

AS HOUSTON CONTINUES TO reach great heights, so too do its residents—whether secured to a building or roped to a specially designed course. Once at the top, the view can be rewarding, as evidenced by the vista that greets visitors to the sky lobby on the 60th floor of the 75-story Chase Tower (PAGES 38 AND 39).

◆ © SCOTT TEVEN PHOTOGRAPHY

© WALTER JIMENEZ

OUSTON INVESTS BOTH MONEY and pride in its architecture. Constructed in 1973, the Houston Industries Building (ABOVE) underwent a thorough renovation in 1996, and its trademark "top hat" design makes it one of the city's most recognizable high-rises.

© WALTER JIMÉNEZ

HOUSTON

▲ © SCOTT TEVEN PHOTOGRAPHY

HOUSTON'S BUILDINGS REFLECT not only the sky and clouds, but also the ongoing renaissance that is revitalizing the city's downtown core.

© JIM OLIVE / STOCKYARD PHOTOS

© ROGER HOLDEN / PHOTOPHILE

© JIM OLIVE / STOCKYARD PHOTOS

Sᴇᴇɴ ꜰʀᴏᴍ Sᴀᴍ Hᴏᴜsᴛᴏɴ Pᴀʀᴋ, the Texaco Heritage Plaza (ᴀʙᴏᴠᴇ), with its baroque stylings and Indian granite flourishes, imposes its vertical presence on the flat Texas landscape. Less vertical but more historical, the Esperson Buildings (ᴏᴘᴘᴏsɪᴛᴇ)—built by Mellie Esperson in memory of her late husband, oil magnate Niels Esperson—add an Italian Renaissance flair to Houston's cityscape.

© JIM OLIVE / STOCKYARD PHOTOS

THE MERCURIAL HUES OF A HOUSTON sunset provide a backdrop for those returning from a hard day of work or play. But some professions demand their workers endure until the first light of sunrise.

© JIM OLIVE / STOCKYARD PHOTOS

▲ © BARRY CHAMPAGNE

▲ © JIM OLIVE / STOCKYARD PHOTOS

© JIM OLIVE / STOCKYARD PHOTOS

FROM ITS HIGH-TECH CONTROL room, Houston Transtar (BOTTOM) oversees transportation operations and traffic conditions for a more than 5,000-square-mile area. But to escape the car-clogged expressways and bypasses, locals can attend ballet, symphony, and opera performances at the 3,000-seat Jesse H. Jones Hall (OPPOSITE BOTTOM).

© JIM OLIVE / STOCKYARD PHOTOS

© SCOTT TEVEN PHOTOGRAPHY

© JANICE RUBIN

© PAT BURON

© JUDI PARKS

© PAMELA SMEDLEY

Jackie Harris' *Fruitmobile* (TOP RIGHT) proves that car art is always in season. As host city to the annual Art Car Parade, Houston certainly enjoys its share. Whether it's Jody Bobrovsky's technicolor Volvo or artist David Best's buffalo-headed, 1984 Camaro *Faith*, an automobile—or even a bike—can become a vehicle for personal expression.

◆ c RAY SOTO PHOTOGRAPHY

© JONATHAN POSTAL / TOWERY PUBLISHING, INC.

COMBINING ART WITH SOCIAL activism, Project Row Houses—founded in 1992 by Rick Lowe (ABOVE)—sponsors artists' shows in its 22 shotgun-style houses in the Third Ward district. An installation of a distinctly different flavor, the Orange Show (OPPOSITE) is a visionary folk art sculpture built single-handedly by Jefferson D. McKissack and dedicated to the many qualities of its namesake fruit.

© DERON NEBLETT

© JANICE RUBIN

© JONATHAN POSTAL / TOWERY PUBLISHING, INC.

© JONATHAN POSTAL / TOWERY PUBLISHING, INC.

VARIETY TRULY IS THE SPICE OF life on Houston's arts scene. The Bobbindoctrin Puppet Theatre, along with its founder, Joel Orr (TOP LEFT), presents puppet shows for adults. Through his latest book, *How to Read a Poem and Fall in Love with Poetry*, Edward Hirsch (BOTTOM LEFT) spreads his love of poetry to readers far beyond Houston's city limits. And Dr. Sidney Berger (BOTTOM RIGHT) founded the Houston Shakespeare Theatre Festival and serves as director of the University of Houston's School of Theatre. For performances by the Houston Grand Opera and the Houston Ballet, patrons head downtown to the Gus S. Wortham Theater Center (OPPOSITE), whose unique, two-stage design accommodates performances by both troupes.

▲ © JUDI PARKS

▲ © JONATHAN POSTAL / TOWERY PUBLISHING, INC.

FEATURING PHOTOGRAPHS FROM around the world, the annual Houston FotoFest benefits from the participation of local attorneys Beverly Ann Young and James Edward Maloney (OPPOSITE). Peter C. Marzio– director of the Museum of Fine Arts, Houston–makes it possible for visitors to view works like Kees van Dongen's *The Corn Poppy* (TOP).

▲ © JUDI PARKS

© JONATHAN POSTAL / TOWERY PUBLISHING, INC.

G RIM REMINDERS OF NAZI ATROCITIES
and loving memorials to the millions of murdered Jews appear
throughout the Holocaust Museum
Houston. On exhibit are paintings by local
artist Alice Lok Cahana (TOP)—a survivor of
both Auschwitz and Bergen-Belsen—who
was featured in the Steven Spielberg-
produced documentary *The Last Days*.

© JONATHAN POSTAL / TOWERY PUBLISHING, INC.

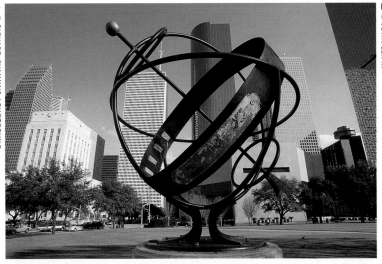

© RICHARD CUMMINS / PHOTOPHILE

© JOHN ELK III

© JIM OLIVE / STOCKYARD PHOTOS

© RICHARD CUMMINS / PHOTOPHILE

W ITH FACILITIES SUCH AS THE Contemporary Arts Museum (OPPOSITE) leading the way, whimsical and often sublime public sculptures abound in Houston. Prominent pieces include the Armillary Sphere in Sam Houston Park (TOP LEFT), Claes Oldenburg's *Geometric Mouse X* (BOTTOM LEFT), Ed Wilson's seasonal *Holiday Wishes for Planet Earth* in Jones Plaza (BOTTOM RIGHT), *Manila Palm: An Oasis Secret* by Mel Chin (OPPOSITE), and Jean Dubuffet's *Monument au Phantome* (PAGES 66 AND 67).

◆ © JIM OLIVE / STOCKYARD PHOTOS

© BIL OLIVE

▲ © BIL OLIVE

BRICK AND MORTAR MAKE FOR AN excellent canvas, where kaleidoscopic colors honor Houston's past and celebrate its present.

© RAY VIATOR

© MARK & JENNIFER MILLER

ALTHOUGH IT DECORATES THE fields along highways throughout Texas, the bluebonnet—the state flower since 1901—also serves an important ecological function: preventing soil erosion. Though much less colorful, cotton has become one of Texas' biggest crops since its introduction in 1745 by Spanish missionaries.

© PAT BURON

© JIM OLIVE / STOCKYARD PHOTOS

FARMERS FROM ALL OVER THE Houston area bring only their freshest fruits and vegetables to sell at places like the Farmer's Market on Airline Drive (OPPOSITE). Beautiful as well as edible, the produce creates a cornucopia of tasty temptations.

© JIM OLIVE / STOCKYARD PHOTOS

▲ © JIM OLIVE / STOCKYARD PHOTOS

HEEDING THE SIREN'S CALL: The toasty-hot dog days of a Houston summer make local establishments like the La Sirenita Bar welcome sights for the thirsty.

© ROGER HOLDEN / PHOTOPHILE

HOUSTON

© SCOTT TEVEN PHOTOGRAPHY

HE ARCHITECTURAL WONDERS around Houston tend to inspire awe in locals and visitors alike. More than 11,000 gallons of water pour down the sides of the Waterwall at Transco Tower (TOP). Located near the famous Warwick Hotel, Hermann Park's Mecom Fountain (BOTTOM) consists of three circular fountains.

© RICHARD CUMMINS / PHOTOPHILE

CITY IN MOTION

© JONATHAN POSTAL / TOWERY PUBLISHING, INC.

© JONATHAN POSTAL / TOWERY PUBLISHING, INC.

CONNOISSEURS WILL FIND HOUSTON a veritable seafood paradise. Just miles from the Gulf of Mexico, the city has access to some of the tastiest salt- and freshwater treats around. And at Tony's (LEFT)—owned by restaurateur Tony Vallone—Chef Bruce McMillan serves up some of the best of them.

© JONATHAN POSTAL / TOWERY PUBLISHING, INC.

MIXING CULTURES AND TRADITIONS in ways both usual and unusual, Houston cuisine proves surprisingly diverse. Irma Galvan (ABOVE) prepares spicy Tex-Mex fare at Irma's, while Scott Chen's, named after its owner and head chef (OPPOSITE), mixes French and Oriental foods with such success that *Esquire* magazine named it one of the country's best new restaurants in 1999.

© SCOTT TEVEN PHOTOGRAPHY

© JUDI PARKS

© SCOTT TEVEN PHOTOGRAPHY

AS PART OF THE HOUSTON LIVESTOCK Show and Rodeo Parade, the Valley Lodge Trail Riders (BOTTOM RIGHT) travel by horse from the Houston Farm and Ranch Club to Memorial Park, where the festivities include roasting quail.

Just as many people arrive via more modern transportation at Kemah, Texas, for seafood at the Brass Parrot (LEFT) or at downtown Houston for the Tex-Mex fare of Cabo (OPPOSITE).

© JUDI PARKS

© JIM OLIVE / STOCKYARD PHOTOS

HOUSTONIANS LOVE THE NIGHTLIFE. When the sun goes down, the city's bustling social scene brings out the gregarious nature of locals as they wine and dine with friends.

© JUDI PARKS

▶ © WALTER JIMÉNEZ

© JONATHAN POSTAL / TOWERY PUBLISHING, INC.

© JIM OLIVE / STOCKYARD PHOTOS

HEADQUARTERED IN A RENOVATED 1924 church, the Aurora Picture Show, a local nonprofit founded by Executive Director Andrea Grover (ABOVE), gives regional filmmakers a hand by sponsoring screenings, lectures, and film festivals. Also spotlighting independ film is the River Oaks Theatre (OPPOSIT which features a packed schedule of a films and midnight movies, including th classic *Rocky Horror Picture Show*.

ECLECTIC AND ENERGIZED, HOUSTON'S music scene encompasses styles ranging from salsa to hip-hop. On 1997 album *Southside Story*, local rap artist Big Mello (RIGHT) chronicles his experiences on the city's streets.

© DERON NEBLETT

◆ © DERON NEBLETT

© JONATHAN POSTAL / TOWERY PUBLISHING, INC.

© JONATHAN POSTAL / TOWERY PUBLISHING, INC.

I N HOUSTON, THE SWING AND ROCKABILLY revivals call for retro threads and flashy dance moves. Local DJ Lucky Larue (OPPOSITE) keeps fans jumpin', jivin', and wailin' as he spins swing records at clubs all around town.

© JONATHAN POSTAL / TOWERY PUBLISHING, INC.

HOUSTON IS A HOTBED OF TEXAS blues, as perfected by Joe "Guitar" Hughes (RIGHT), who has been slinging guitar riffs for more than four decades. Taking cues from fellow Texan Janis Joplin, Carolyn Wonderland (LEFT) fronts the Imperial Monkeys on albums like *Bursting with Flavor* and *Play with Matches*. Eschewing the blues for early rock and roll, Chadd Thomas and the Crazy Kings (OPPOSITE) specialize in updating yesterday's guitar-driven rockabilly shuffles

▲ © SCOTT TEVEN PHOTOGRAPHY

▲ © JANICE RUBIN

▲ © JIM OLIVE / STOCKYARD PHOTOS

© BARRY CHAMPAGNE

ACCORDIONS AND BANJOS PREVAIL throughout Houston, as zydeco and bluegrass strike a chord with many music lovers. Held every spring, the Houston International Festival features music from performers such as Nathan Williams and the Zydeco Cha Chas (OPPOSITE TOP). Bluegrass is growing in popularity as well, thanks to some extremely talented local musicians.

© JIM OLIVE / STOCKYARD PHOTOS

© JUDI PARKS

© JUDI PARKS

NOT MERELY AN EXCUSE FOR outrageousness and flamboyance, Galveston's Mardi Gras celebrations date back to 1867 and attract hundreds of thousands of visitors from across the country, including the 14-and-under members of the Krewe of Munchkins (RIGHT).

© JUDI PARKS

© JUDI PARKS

© JUDI PARKS

© JUDI PARKS

FOR A GLIMPSE OF PERSONAL FORTUNES, some Houstonians frequent the city's psychics and palm readers. Attendees at the annual Mardi Gras parade (OPPOSITE) anticipate a future within reach as they vie for souvenir beads to commemorate the occasion.

© JUDI PARKS

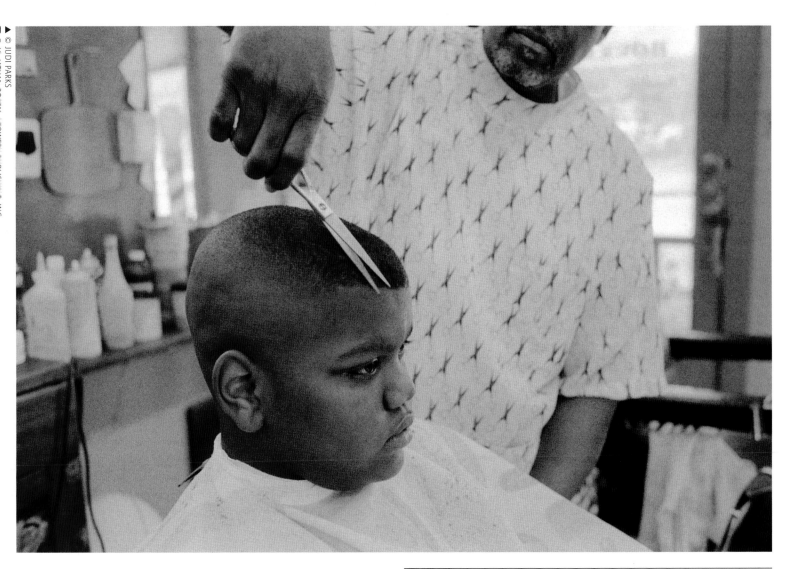

© JUDI PARKS

A LITTLE SNIP HERE AND SOME hair spray there and you've got yourself a new 'do. And although some opt for a close shave to beat Houston's unrelenting heat, others revel in a towering bouffant—one of the many specialties at Venus Hair Salon, where Susan Venus (OPPOSITE, ON LEFT) and Susan Romeo (ON RIGHT) pilot the clippers.

© JIM OLIVE / STOCKYARD PHOTOS

© JIM OLIVE / STOCKYARD PHOTOS

AT THE HOUSTON GALLERIA, THE famed Neiman Marcus department store rolls out the red carpet for all its shoppers. No matter what the weather might bring, visitors can always chill out on the shopping mall's ice-skating rink.

© JONATHAN POSTAL / TOWERY PUBLISHING, INC.

© JONATHAN POSTAL / TOWERY PUBLISHING, INC.

F EW KNOW FASHION AS WELL AS Lucho Flores (LEFT), owner of Houston's premier menswear emporium–appropriately named Lucho– and a tireless rainforest activist. Houston native Selven O'Keef Jarmon (OPPOSITE) is a rising star in his own right and is making a name for himself in the design world both locally and nationally.

© JIM OLIVE / STOCKYARD PHOTOS

▲ © JUDI PARKS

IN PRESENT-DAY HOUSTON, JUST as in the Old West, clothes make the cowboy—and the cowgirl, as well. The several Boot Town stores around the city offer all the trappings of western style, from snakeskin boots and duster jackets to calfskin vests and denims.

▲ © JUDI PARKS

© JUDI PARKS

© RAY SOTO PHOTOGRAPHY

© SCOTT TEVEN PHOTOGRAPHY

© JONATHAN POSTAL / TOWERY PUBLISHING, INC.

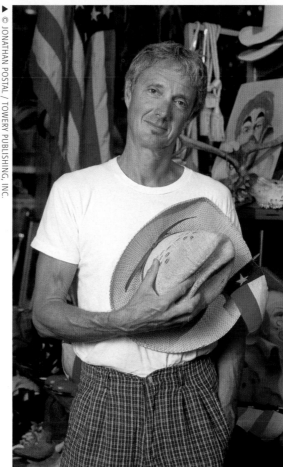

INGER LYLE LOVETT SAID IT BEST: "You can have my girl, but don't touch my hat." Symbolizing the spirit and pride of Texas, the cowboy hat is a highly valued personal possession treasured by many a Texan. But if it's vintage you crave, check out the Texas Junk Company, where Bob Novotney (BOTTOM RIGHT) sells hats and boots that have improved with age.

▼ © JONATHAN POSTAL / TOWERY PUBLISHING, INC.

▼ © JONATHAN POSTAL / TOWERY PUBLISHING, INC.

SCOTT TELEK PHOTOGRAPHY

OLD-TIME COWBOYS MIGHT GRIMAC at the thought of a smooch from a beautiful cowgirl, but a new generation of pardners isn't shy about lassoing a member of the opposite sex.

© JIM OLIVE / STOCKYARD PHOTOS

Once called the Eighth Wonder of the World, the Houston Astrodome became notorious as the first indoor baseball stadium in major-league history—even as many purists scoffed at its Astroturf field and air-conditioned climate. While the Astros have moved over to the new Enron Field, their old facility still hosts a full roster of sporting and rodeo events.

© SCOTT TEVEN PHOTOGRAPHY

THE RODEO HAS EVOLVED FROM a friendly roping contest among cowboys to a full-fledged sport with its own star athletes. Locally, events like RodeoHouston draw thousands of fans to spur on the riders.

© JIM OLIVE / STOCKYARD PHOTOS
© RAY SOTO PHOTOGRAPHY

ALTHOUGH THEIR OWNERS WIN the top prizes, the animals usually hog the glory each year at the Houston Livestock Show and Rodeo. Held in the Astrohall, the event showcases nearly 40,000 professional and junior exhibitors and their top animals—from cattle and sheep to chickens and rabbits—all of which bask in the attention of more than 12,000 volunteers and nearly 2 million attendants.

© JONATHAN POSTAL / TOWERY PUBLISHING, INC.

© JONATHAN POSTAL / TOWERY PUBLISHING, INC.

THE 500-ACRE GEORGE RANCH Historical Park traces more than a century of Texas history. Re-creating cattle-working and farming techniques of the 1800s and early 1900s, the park provides visitors with a glimpse of life in the days of the A.P. George family, whose 23,000-acre ranch is still in operation.

© SCOTT TEVEN PHOTOGRAPHY

© RAY SOTO PHOTOGRAPHY

© JIM OLIVE / STOCKYARD PHOTOS

© JIM OLIVE / STOCKYARD PHOTOS

© JONATHAN POSTAL / TOWERY PUBLISHING, INC.

O NCE THE AREA'S PRIMARY MODE of transportation, the horse still takes center stage in Houston today. Whether on the ranch, race track, polo field, or city streets, the sturdy steed has a secure spot in Texas lore.

© ROBERT LABERGE / ALLSPORT USA

© JON FERREY / ALLSPORT USA

DURING THE ONE EVENT IN HOUSTON when speeding is not only legal but encouraged, professional Championship Auto Racing Teams (CART) drivers take to the streets for the annual Texaco Grand Prix of Houston. The event draws nearly 60,000 fans, some of whom can be enamored with the swift celebrities. A busy racer with a tight schedule, Christian Fittipaldi had to turn down this invitation (TOP).

© JIM OLIVE / STOCKYARD PHOTOS

© JIM OLIVE / STOCKYARD PHOTOS

© JIM OLIVE / STOCKYARD PHOTOS

© JIM OLIVE / STOCKYARD PHOTOS

G REETED BY LOONEY TUNES characters Bugs Bunny and Tweety, visitors to Houston's Six Flags Astroworld amusement park usually head straight for the Texas Tornado (OPPOSITE). The whirlwind-inspired dervish, one of the state's most popular roller coasters, loops and plunges at speeds of more than 60 miles per hour.

▼ © PAT BURON

© BRUCE GLASS

© SCOTT TEVEN PHOTOGRAPHY

AFTER BUILDING UP THEIR STAMINA racing bicycles at the Alkek Velodrome in Cullen Park (BOTTOM) and diving right into swim training at the Woodlands Athletic Center's diving tank (OPPOSITE), Houston's athletes should be ready to endure any competition.

© BRIAN BAHR / ALLSPORT USA

© JIM OLIVE / STOCKYARD PHOTOS

© BRIAN BAHR / ALLSPORT USA

FOR THE START OF THE 2000 season, the Houston Astros moved from the historic Astrodome to the new Enron Field. Named for the locally based Enron Corporation, the park features an 18-million-pound retractable roof, which takes approximately 12 minutes to open and allows for both indoor and open-air games. During its first season, Enron Field hosted more than 2.5 million fans—an increase of almost 500,000 people from the Astros' previous season.

© JIM OLIVE / STOCKYARD PHOTOS

▼ © JIM OLIVE / STOCKYARD PHOTOS

© HARRY HOW / ALLSPORT USA

HOUSTON'S AVID GOLFERS GET teed off if they can't play their favorite sport. To keep them happy, the city has more than 30 golf courses and hosts several tournaments each year, including the Shell Open (ABOVE) at the Woodlands. A variation of the classic pastime, Frisbee golf (OPPOSITE) is growing in popularity among a younger set of players.

© JONATHAN POSTAL / TOWERY PUBLISHING, INC.

© JONATHAN POSTAL / TOWERY PUBLISHING, INC.

BOXING HAS ALWAYS HAD A MODEST following locally, but the sport received a boost when Houston pugilist Rocky Juarez (ABOVE LEFT) repre- sented the city at the 2000 Olympics in Sydney. Like many talented local fighters, Juarez trains at Ray's Boxing Club.

© RICHARD CUMMINS / PHOTOPHILE

© JUDI PARKS

© TOM ARLEDGE / PHOTOPHILE

© JIM OLIVE / STOCKYARD PHOTOS

HOUSTON OFFERS ITS CHILDREN many opportunities to hit home runs, shoot baskets, and kick goals. But for most kids, playing sports is less about the athletic experience than it is about the simple fun of it all.

▲ © JIM OLIVE / STOCKYARD PHOTOS
© SCOTT TEVEN PHOTOGRAPHY

J OGGING PROVIDES AN OPPORTUNITY
to leave the rat race behind in favor
of the foot race. Places like Houston's

© JIM OLIVE / STOCKYARD PHOTOS

© JIM OLIVE / STOCKYARD PHOTOS

© RAY SOTO PHOTOGRAPHY

© WALTER JIMÉNEZ

© JIM OLIVE / STOCKYARD PHOTOS

THE OLD ADAGE THAT EVERYTHING is big in Texas certainly applies to some of Houston's mansions, which reflect the city's sense of style and grandeur. Many come with the usual amenities—swimming pools, tennis courts, well-manicured lawns—while others feature accoutrements as unique as the architecture itself.

© PAMELA SMEDLEY

© PAMELA SMEDLEY

© PAMELA SMEDLEY

KNOCK, KNOCK, KNOCKIN' ON Houston's doors: With or without adornments, the entrances to the city's homes are symbolic of Houston's welcoming spirit and warm hospitality.

© PAMELA SMEDLEY

© PAMELA SMEDLEY

© MARK E. GIBSON / PHOTOPHILE
© MARK E. GIBSON / PHOTOPHILE

RAWING MORE THAN 3,000 undergraduate and graduate students, Rice University is situated on a 285-acre campus amid approximately 4,000 trees. With 50 buildings designed in the institution's trademark neo-Byzantine style, the campus offers an environment conducive to studying.

© JIM OLIVE / STOCKYARD PHOTOS

© RAY SOTO PHOTOGRAPHY

ALTHOUGH THE HOUSTON MUSEUM of Natural Science was founded in 1909, many of the exhibits it houses date back millions of years. Today, it is the fourth-most-visited museum in the country, arousing the curiosity of more than 2 million visitors each year.

© JONATHAN POSTAL / TOWERY PUBLISHING, INC.

© RICHARD CUMMINS / PHOTOPHILE

EXPERTS AT THE HOUSTON MUSEUM of Natural Science can discern a great deal of useful information from the skeleton of an ancient fish (TOP). Founded in 1997, the city's Museum of Health and Medical Science allows visitors to bone up on their knowledge of the human body through a number of innovative exhibits (BOTTOM). But on the city's outskirts, the remains of longhorns (OPPOSITE) serve simply as a Texas-style greeting.

© RICHARD CUMMINS / PHOTOPHILE

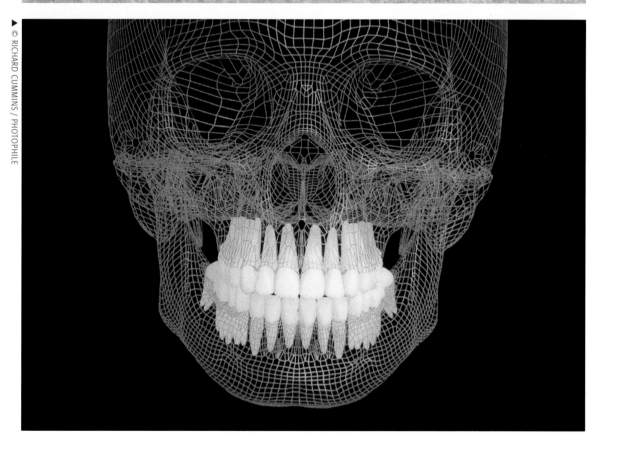

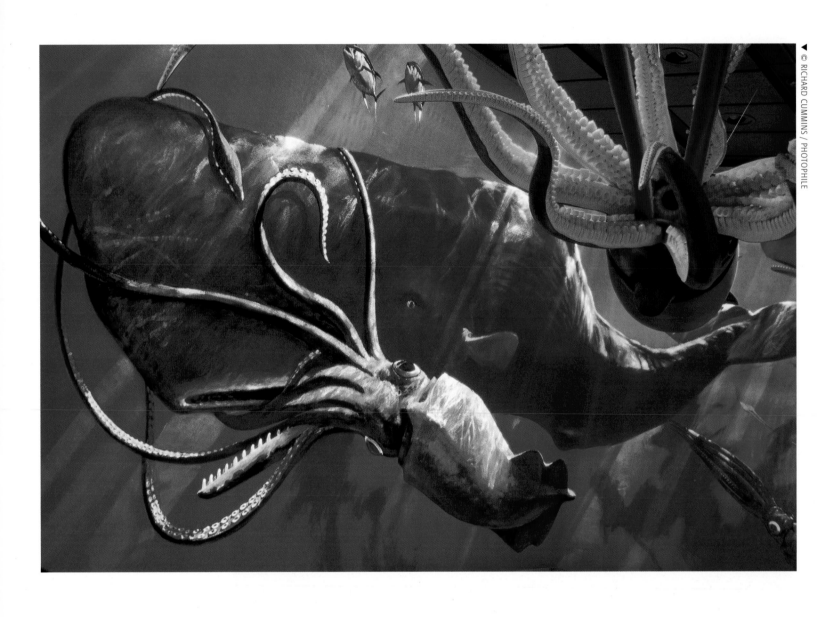

© RICHARD CUMMINS / PHOTOPHILE

© PAT BURON

HOUSTON CERTAINLY HAS ITS SHARE of creature discomforts. The Foley's Thanksgiving Parade features a frightening replica of King Kong (ABOVE). At the Museum of Natural Science (OPPOSITE), it's a mural depiction of the undersea world that proves so very menacing.

▼ © BIL OLIVE

▼ © BIL OLIVE

▲ © JUDI PARKS

▲ © SCOTT TEVEN PHOTOGRAPHY

DURING THE DOG DAYS OF SUMMER, many Houstonians crave a little canine companionship, and some even turn their puppy love into a full-time hobby. Doris Lee (BOTTOM) created the Bull Dog Car in honor of her beloved pet. But dogs aren't the only animals over which Texans obsess: The horse has long been associated with cowboys of the Old West (PAGE 152), as has the fictitious—but always funny—jackalope (PAGE 153).

◆ © JIM OLIVE / STOCKYARD PHOTOS

◆ © JONATHAN POSTAL / TOWERY PUBLISHING, INC.

© RAY SOTO PHOTOGRAPHY

© PURCELL TEAM / HILLSTROM STOCK PHOTO

© JIM OLIVE / STOCKYARD PHOTOS

THERE'S A VERITABLE ANIMAL KINGDOM awaiting visitors to some of Houston's most popular attractions. The crowds get all a-flutter over the winged delights of the Cockrell Butterfly Center (TOP). The Houston Zoological Gardens occupies 55 acres near downtown and is home to some 5,000 animals, the noble lion among them (OPPOSITE). In the small town of High Island (BOTTOM), birdwatchers can observe several species of avifauna at two separate sites managed by the Houston Audubon Society. But for something that's much easier to spot, locals can venture over to Clear Lake for the Ballunar Liftoff Festival, which features more than 100 hot-air balloons (PAGES 156 AND 157).

◆ © BARRY CHAMPAGNE

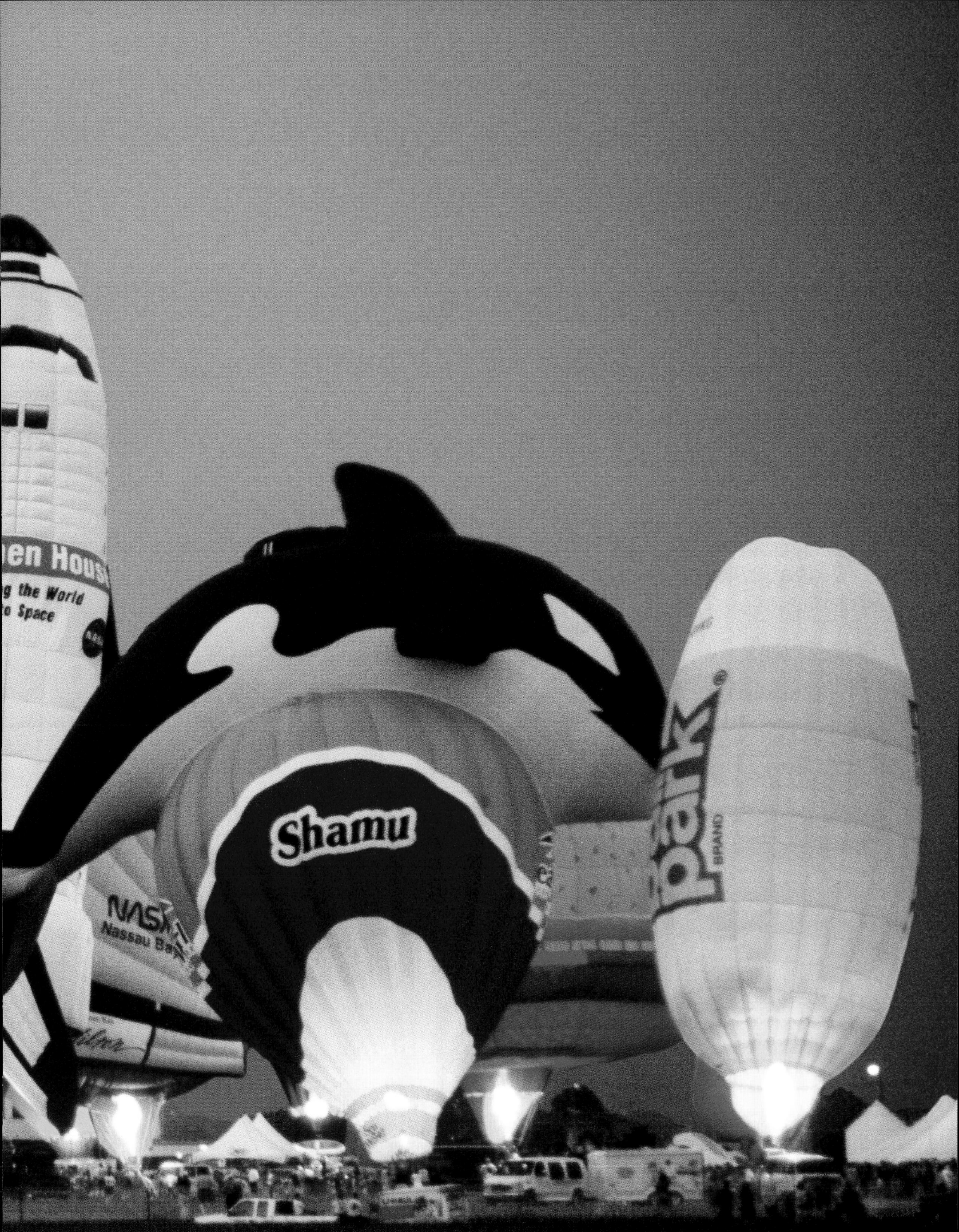
Shamu
NASA
Nassau Bay
BRAND

© JIM OLIVE / STOCKYARD PHOTOS

© JOHN FIK III

© JIM OLIVE / STOCKYARD PHOTOS

WHEN IT OPENED IN 1963, the Manned Spacecraft Center was the heart of the United States' heated space race with the U.S.S.R. Now known as the Lyndon B. Johnson Space Center, the facility remains integral to space exploration efforts, drawing thousands of visitors each year to see life-size models of spacecraft such as the Saturn V (OPPOSITE).

◆ © JIM OLIVE / STOCKYARD PHOTOS

© JIM OLIVE / STOCKYARD PHOTOS

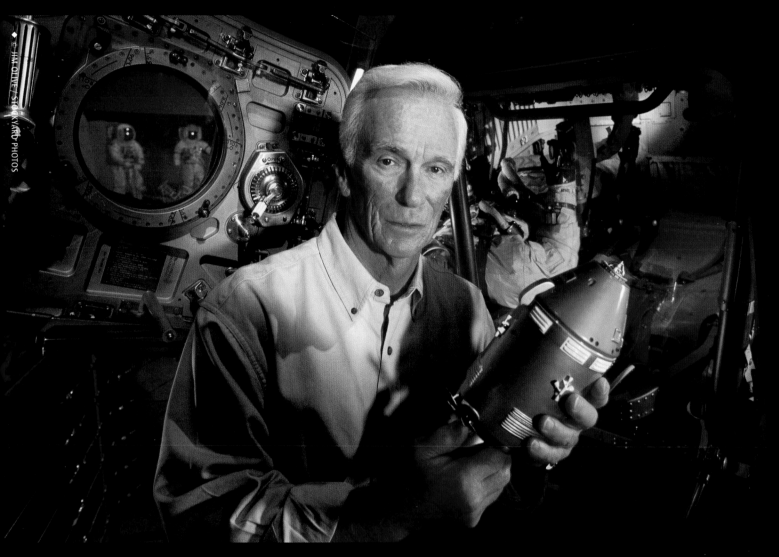

FORMER ASTRONAUT EUGENE CERNAN (ABOVE) is considered the last person to set foot on the Moon. In 1972, he commanded Apollo 17, NASA's final manned lunar mission. Then, as now, Mission Control (OPPOSITE) at Johnson Space Center tracks every detail as spacecraft hurtle through space.

© JIM OLIVE / STOCKYARD PHOTOS

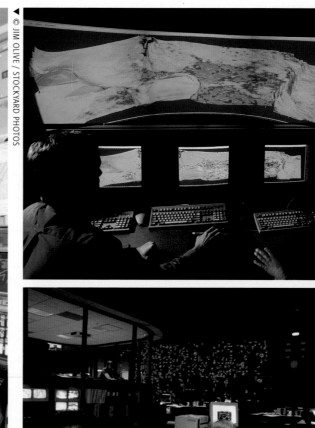

© JANICE RUBIN

© JIM OLIVE / STOCKYARD PHOTOS

© JIM OLIVE / STOCKYARD PHOTOS

INNOVATIONS ARE PART OF EVERY day for Houston's businesses and schools. From the Rice School/La Escuela Rice program—a collaboration between the Houston Independent School District and Rice University (ABOVE)—to astronauts piloting complex spacecraft, the region is at the forefront of technological advances.

© JONATHAN POSTAL / TOWERY PUBLISHING, INC.

© JONATHAN POSTAL / TOWERY PUBLISHING, INC.

I N 1996, RICE UNIVERSITY PROFESSORS Dr. Robert F. Curl Jr. and Dr. Richard E. Smalley (ABOVE) were awarded the Nobel Prize in Chemistry for their discovery of carbon molecules shaped like soccer balls. Conducting equally important research is Dr. John Mendelsohn, president of the University of Texas M.D. Anderson Cancer Center.

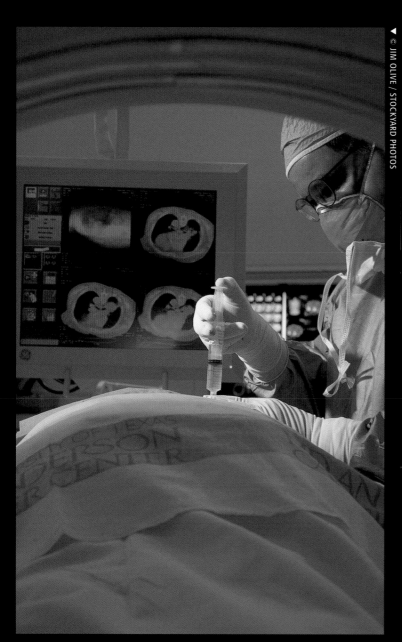

© JIM OLIVE / STOCKYARD PHOTOS

© JIM OLIVE / STOCKYARD PHOTOS

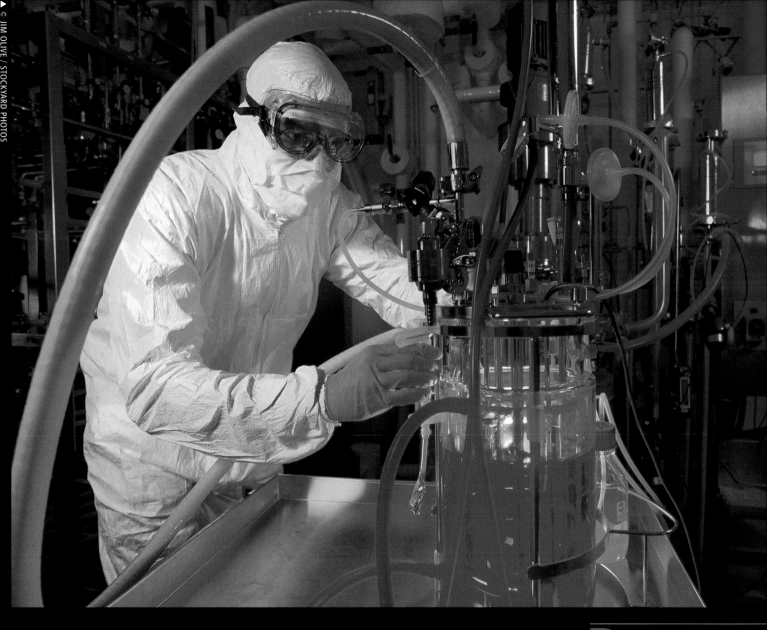

© JIM OLIVE / STOCKYARD PHOTOS

DRIVEN BY ITS MISSION TO TREAT cancer patients more efficiently and more effectively, Houston's M.D. Anderson Cancer Center has been ranked first in the nation for cancer care by *U.S. News & World Report.*

© JANICE RUBIN

THROUGHOUT THE HOUSTON REGION, the Texas Medical Center has more than 40 research and health care institutions, which serve almost 5 million patients annually. A true legend in this medical arena, Michael DeBakey (OPPOSITE) performed the first successful coronary bypass in 1964.

▼ © JIM OLIVE / STOCKYARD PHOTOS

© JONATHAN POSTAL / TOWERY PUBLISHING, INC.

A HANDFUL OF HOUSTONIANS ARE gifted with the ability to carve lifelike images from various media. Sculpting on a grand scale, David Adickes (ABOVE) creates larger-than-life likenesses of the state's biggest legends.

In the digital realm, Geary Broadnax (OPPOSITE) cofounded Insync Internet Services, which provides business-to-business Internet service and was recently purchased by industry giant Reliant Energy Communications.

© RAY VIATOR

© RAY VIATOR

IMAGES OF LEGENDARY TEXAN SAM Houston abound throughout the region, but none stand as tall as David Adickes' 67-foot statue in Huntsville (OPPOSITE).

© RAY SOTO PHOTOGRAPHY

© RICHARD CUMMINS / PHOTOPHILE

HOUSTON

© SCOTT TEVEN PHOTOGRAPHY

THROUGH STIRRING MONUMENTS and remembrances, Houston honors its soldiers killed during battle, as well as those who survived. The Moving Wall (ABOVE), a small-scale version of the Vietnam Memorial in Washington, D.C., visited the University of Houston campus in November 1999, drawing hundreds of veterans from around the area. Dedicated on Veteran's Day, 1995, the U.S.S. *Houston* Monument (OPPOSITE RIGHT) in Sam Houston Park memorializes the ship and its crew of more than 1,000 men, who were either drowned or captured when the ship was sunk in 1942. Rising prominently from the San Jacinto Battleground State Historical Park, the San Jacinto Monument (OPPOSITE LEFT) commemorates the famous battle that led to Texas' independence from Mexico.

© RAY SOTO PHOTOGRAPHY

HOUSTON

© RICHARD CUMMINS / PHOTOPHILE

© JOHN ELK III

PARADES AND EXHIBITS PAY TRIBUTE to Texas' past and present. Galveston's Lone Star Flight Museum displays more than 40 World War II aircraft (TOP), while the *Battleship Texas*, which served in both world wars, is permanently docked near San Jacinto State Historical Park.

© JIM OLIVE / STOCKYARD PHOTOS

© JIM OLIVE / STOCKYARD PHOTOS

© SCOTT TEVEN PHOTOGRAPHY

RED, WHITE, AND HOUSTON: WHILE the sizes of the flags vary from small to very large, the colors remain the same as the city displays its patriotic fervor. Both the stars and stripes and the Texas state flag—which echoes the national color scheme—often show up in unexpected places: on the faces of young celebrants; in neon (PAGE 180 AND 181); and, along with many others, in an installation of spike lights for the Houston Economic Summit (PAGES 182 AND 183).

© RICHARD CUMMINS / PHOTOPHILE

◆ © JIM OLIVE / STOCKYARD PHOTOS

FOUR
SEASONS
HOTEL

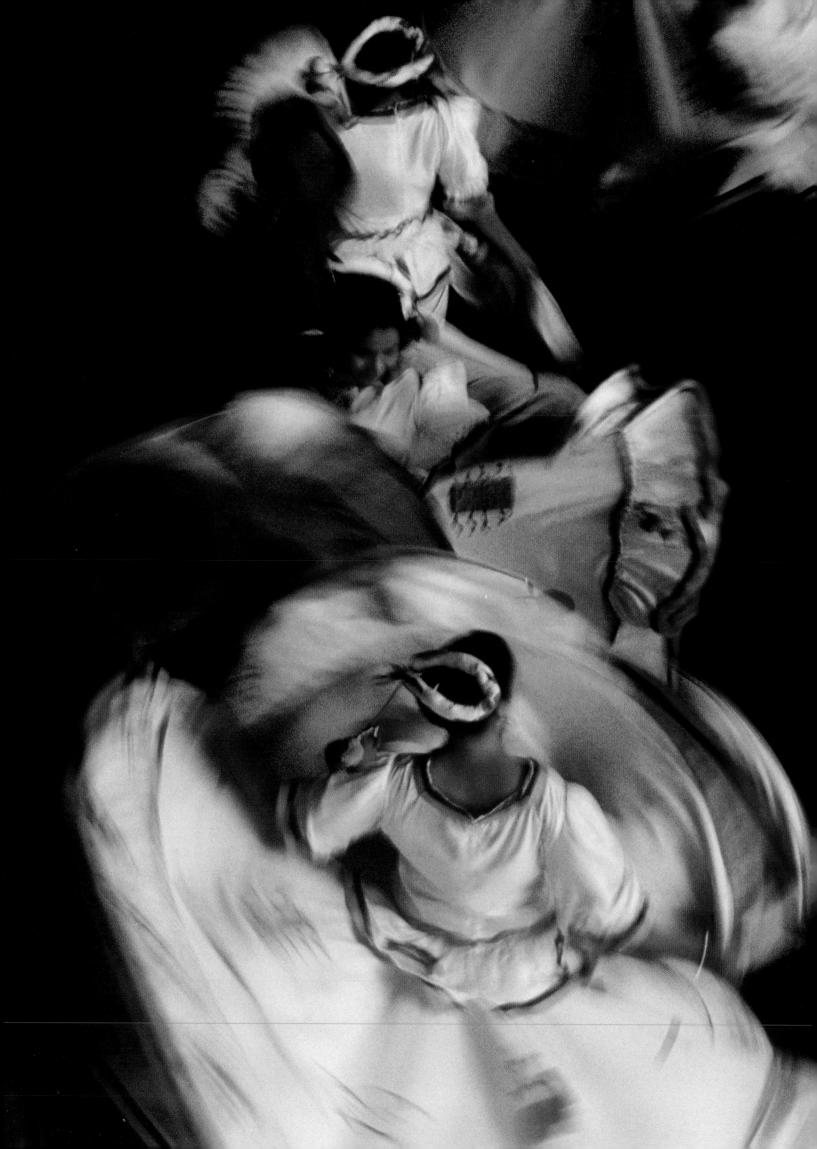

© SCOTT TEVEN PHOTOGRAPHY

THE WHIRLING COLORS OF CELE-
bratory costumes can mean only
one thing: It's party time in
Houston. From Cinco de Mayo to the
annual Houston International Festival,
the city pays tribute to its cultural diversity.

© SCOTT TEVEN PHOTOGRAPHY

© RAY SOTO PHOTOGRAPHY

© RAY SOTO PHOTOGRAPHY

© RAY SOTO PHOTOGRAPHY

HOUSTON'S EXTENSIVE SCHEDULE of cultural festivals reflects its strikingly multiethnic population. Marked on every calendar are celebrations of African-American, Italian, Indian, Japanese, Chinese, and Greek cultures, among many others.

© JIM OLIVE / STOCKYARD PHOTOS

THE TEXAS GUANDI TEMPLE (OPPOSITE) represents just one example of the wealth of spiritualities found in Houston's Asian neighborhoods—where the street signs are printed in both Chinese and English.

© JONATHAN POSTAL / TOWERY PUBLISHING, INC.

© BUDGET TEAM / HILLSTROM STOCK PHOTO

FROM STEEPLES AND TOWERS TO domes and crosses (PAGES 190-193), Houston's houses of worship reflect a spectrum of beliefs and a variety of architectural approaches. Churches and cathedrals like St. Paul's United Methodist Church (ABOVE), designed by local architect Nicholas Clayton, and Annunciation Catholic Church (OPPOSITE), one of the oldest churches in Houston, foster the city's spirituality with open arms.

◆ © RAY VIATOR

HOUSTON

© JONATHAN POSTAL / TOWERY PUBLISHING, INC.

ONNECTING BAYTOWN AND LAPORTE, the Fred Hartman Bridge—with its graceful spires and trademark yellow suspension cables—stands tall as a modern addition to the Houston Ship Channel riverscape. An architectural landmark, the bridge received the American Society of Civil Engineers' 1996 award for Outstanding Civil Engineering Achievement.

© JIM OLIVE / STOCKYARD PHOTOS

◆ C RAY SOTO PHOTOGRAPHY

14 M
B
6
4

◆ © RAY SOTO PHOTOGRAPHY

© JIM OLIVE / STOCKYARD PHOTOS

© JIM OLIVE / STOCKYARD PHOTOS

THE 25-MILE PORT OF HOUSTON handles approximately 170 million tons of cargo, and docks nearly 7,000 cargo ships annually (PAGES 196-199). Ranked first in the nation for foreign tonnage and second for total tonnage, the port has a tremendous impact on the region's economy and industry, creating thousands of jobs and billions of dollars in revenue.

© RAY SOTO PHOTOGRAPHY
© JIM OLIVE / STOCKYARD PHOTOS

CONSTRUCTED IN 1914, THE HOUSTON Ship Channel runs 52 miles, connecting the city with the Gulf of Mexico. The constant activity along the waterway readily affirms Houston's status as a city in motion.

◆ © BARRY CHAMPAGNE

© RICHARD CUMMINS / PHOTOPHILE

◆ © JIM OLIVE / STOCKYARD PHOTOS

© JIM OLIVE / STOCKYARD PHOTOS

CITY IN MOTION

HOUSTON

A LOOK AT THE CORPORATIONS, BUSINESSES, PROFESSIONAL GROUPS, AND COMMUNITY SERVICE ORGANIZATIONS THAT HAVE MADE THIS BOOK POSSIBLE. THEIR STORIES—OFFERING AN INFORMAL CHRONICLE OF THE LOCAL BUSINESS COMMUNITY—ARE ARRANGED ACCORDING TO THE DATE THEY WERE ESTABLISHED IN THE HOUSTON AREA.

ANDERSEN CONSULTING ● THE ART INSTITUTE OF HOUSTON ● BAYKO GIBSON CARNEGIE & HAGAN LLP ● BOYAR & MILLER ● CELANESE CHEMICALS CLEAR LAKE PLANT ● CITY OF NASSAU BAY ● CLEAR LAKE AREA ECONOMIC DEVELOPMENT FOUNDATION ● THE DIOCESE OF GALVESTON-HOUSTON ● DOUBLETREE HOTEL AT POST OAK ● DREYER'S GRAND ICE CREAM ● FORT BEND CHAMBER OF COMMERCE ● FRONT OFFICE BUSINESS CENTERS ● GREATER SOUTHWEST HOUSTON CHAMBER OF COMMERCE ● HALLIBURTON COMPANY ● HOUSTON BUSINESS JOURNAL ● HOUSTON COCA-COLA BOTTLING COMPANY ● HOUSTON COMMUNITY COLLEGE SYSTEM ● HOUSTON FEDERAL CREDIT UNION ● HOUSTON GRAND OPERA ● HOUSTON HISPANIC CHAMBER OF COMMERCE ● HOUSTON WEST CHAMBER OF COMMERCE ● LORANCE & THOMPSON, P.C. ● NORTH HARRIS MONTGOMERY COMMUNITY COLLEGE DISTRICT ● THE PEPSI BOTTLING GROUP OF HOUSTON ● PTI, INCORPORATED ● ST. AGNES BAPTIST CHURCH ● SHELL EMPLOYEES FEDERAL CREDIT UNION ● STEWART & STEVENSON ● TEXAS ASSOCIATION OF BUSINESS & CHAMBERS OF COMMERCE ● TEXAS SOUTHERN UNIVERSITY ● TURNER CONSTRUCTION ● UNITY NATIONAL BANK ● UNIVERSITY OF ST. THOMAS ● THE UNIVERSITY OF TEXAS M. D. ANDERSON CANCER CENTER ● WHEELER AVENUE BAPTIST CHURCH ● WICKLIFF & HALL, PC ●

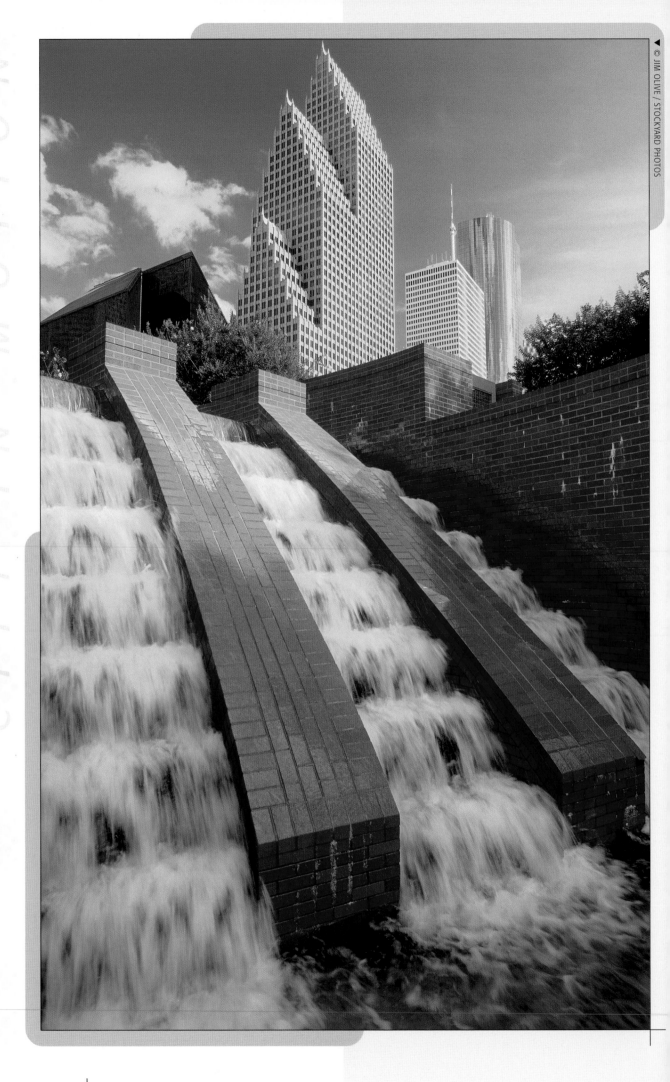

© JIM OLIVE / STOCKYARD PHOTOS

CITY IN MOTION

HOUSTON

1842

THE DIOCESE OF GALVESTON-HOUSTON

1902

HOUSTON COCA-COLA BOTTLING COMPANY

1902

STEWART & STEVENSON

1919

HALLIBURTON COMPANY

1922

TEXAS ASSOCIATION OF
  BUSINESS & CHAMBERS OF COMMERCE

1935

SHELL EMPLOYEES FEDERAL CREDIT UNION

1939

THE PEPSI BOTTLING GROUP OF HOUSTON

1941

THE UNIVERSITY OF TEXAS
  M. D. ANDERSON CANCER CENTER

1947

TEXAS SOUTHERN UNIVERSITY

1947

UNIVERSITY OF ST. THOMAS

1949

GREATER SOUTHWEST HOUSTON
  CHAMBER OF COMMERCE

1955

HOUSTON GRAND OPERA

The Diocese of Galveston-Houston

The Catholic Church has had a presence in Texas since the state's pioneer days, serving as a cornerstone in the development of the Houston-Galveston area long before Texas won independence from Mexico. More than 100 years before the region became the Republic of Texas in 1836, mission churches served by Franciscan priests dotted the land. Many of these beautiful churches still stand, especially in San Antonio, where some continue to serve as active parishes. It was not until 1842 that a bishop was assigned to Galveston, thus beginning the modern history of the Catholic Church in Texas. ● From Galveston, Bishop

Jean Marie Odin ministered to 20,000 Catholics throughout Texas, and over the course of 158 years, the territory that once embraced the Diocese of Galveston has been divided into 16 Catholic dioceses. Today, these 16 dioceses serve 5 million Catholic Texans.

In 1959, the Diocese of Galveston was re-designated the Diocese of Galveston-Houston. It is the largest Texas diocese, with 1.3 million Catholics in 151 parishes, serving a multiethnic, multicultural, and multi-language population. "There are so many facets to our diocese. We are a people

From top:
Sacred Heart Co-Cathedral was established in 1896. The Co-Cathedral is located in downtown Houston, in the heart of the 10-county diocese.

Bishop Joseph A. Fiorenza visits with students at St. Charles Borromeo Elementary, one of the 61 schools in the Diocese of Galveston-Houston which is dedicated to the development of the Christian individual's moral, intellectual, social, and cultural endowments.

A United Way agency, Associated Catholic Charities provides culturally sensitive social services to those in need, without regard to race, religion, or socioeconomic status.

of faith who reach out to the community in many ways—education, charity, and health care," says Bishop Joseph A. Fiorenza.

Faith-based Education

More than 17,350 students attend the 61 schools of the diocese, including seven high schools in Houston and one in Galveston. All schools are fully accredited with the Texas Education Agency—through the Texas Catholic Conference Accreditation Commission—and with the National Catholic Education Association. The educational ministry of the Catholic Church is dedicated to the development of the Christian individual's moral, intellectual, social, and cultural endowments.

The Catholic elementary schools are parish-centered, reflecting the unique qualities of the individual communities in which they are located. The programs in all the schools follow a basic curriculum designed to meet and challenge students' talents and abilities. "The schools are diverse and unique in their educational styles. Within this diversity there is commonality of purpose; the Catholic schools are committed to Christian values and the faith development of students," Fiorenza says.

Devotion to the Community

Helping people in need achieve self-sufficiency is the inspiration for the diocese's Associated Catholic Charities (ACC). A United Way agency, ACC provides culturally sensitive social services to those in need, without regard to race,

religion, or socioeconomic status. As an advocate for social justice, ACC empowers the community through action and education, asserting the principle of human dignity. Proactive response to the needs of the community guides the organization's growth and development. Some of the community needs addressed by ACC include AIDS ministry, adoption services, and immigration services.

ACC recently moved into its new central program facility on Louisiana Street in downtown Houston. The building houses most of the major programs of ACC and also includes training rooms, conference areas, and a meditation room. "The facility is designed to take ACC into the 21st century with increased service capacity, space, and the most current technology," says Julie Platek, vice president of Fund Development and Marketing.

Also working for the health and well-being of the community are the Catholic-sponsored hospitals located in the diocese—St. Joseph, founded in 1887 in downtown Houston; St. John, in Nassau Bay; and St. Catherine, in Katy. All are part of CHRISTUS Health, a faith-based health and wellness ministry comprising more than 30 hospitals and long-term care facilities, as well as dozens of other health services in more than 60 communities in Texas, Arkansas, Louisiana, and Utah. CHRISTUS is sponsored jointly by the congregations of The Sisters of Charity of the Incarnate Word in Houston and The Sisters of Charity of the Incarnate Word in San Antonio.

Millennium Challenge

Fiorenza says the Catholic Church will draw on the strength of its past to guide the future. "Houston, blessed with a good economy, continues to attract people from Mexico, Central America, and Asia, as well as from all parts of the United States. The challenge of the Catholic Church in this millennium will be to minister to this diverse congregation with the same apostolic zeal that motivated the Franciscan priests to face enormous obstacles to bring the gospel of Jesus Christ to Texas in the early 1700s," says Fiorenza.

"Today, the Church faces different obstacles, which are just as daunting, especially with the attitude of modern people who think they do not really need God," says Fiorenza. "This eclipse of God from modern life causes people to ignore God. The Church in this millennium must not allow God to be ignored, but must proclaim his teachings and values so that our world can embrace the truth of God, as did the founders of the nation. The Church has a message for the people of the third millennium that is as necessary and relevant as the modern technology which characterizes the present and the future."

St. Mary's Seminary has been preparing men for the priesthood in the Diocese of Galveston-Houston since October 1901.

St. Catherine is one of more than 30 hospitals and long-term care facilities comprising CHRISTUS Health, a faith-based health and wellness ministry.

Houston Coca-Cola Bottling Company

It's the world's most popular soft drink, requested more than 300 million times daily in at least 155 countries. Its classic bottle ranks among the most recognized trademarks in history. Over the past century, its name has become synonymous with superior quality and taste. Yet when Dr. John Pemberton, an Atlanta pharmacist, created Coca-Cola, he didn't have a beverage in mind. He promoted the syrup as a medicine. Later, a fountain operator accidentally mixed the syrup with carbonated water, and the world's first soft drink was born. ● Coca-Cola's popularity grew after 1899, when Joseph B. Whitehead and Benjamin F. Thomas of Chattanooga, Tennessee, acquired exclusive rights to bottle and sell the soft drink. With another Chattanooga businessman, John T. Lupton, they began building a nationwide bottling network by granting franchise rights to other entrepreneurs. Consolidation of these operations began in the late 1970s. One of the most prominent mergers resulted in the formation of Coca-Cola Enterprises Inc. in 1986.

Coca-Cola Enterprises continued to consolidate America's soft drink business. After merging with Johnson Coca-Cola Bottling Group Inc. in 1991, Coca-Cola Enterprises began a $152 million restructuring and decentralization program to enhance its responsiveness to customers.

Today, Coca-Cola Enterprises operates in 46 states, the District of Columbia, the U.S. Virgin Islands, the Netherlands, the West Indies, and 10 provinces of Canada, as well as Belgium, France, Great Britain, and Luxembourg. The world's largest bottler of Coca-Cola products, the company collaborates closely with its co-owner and business partner, the Coca-Cola Company, which develops products, sells concentrates, and creates advertising campaigns.

A Houston Heritage

Like its parent company, the Houston Coca-Cola Bottling Company has a rich heritage. After opening in 1902, it made deliveries on mule-drawn wagons from its plant northwest of downtown Houston. A decade later, the growing organization relocated to larger quarters.

Rationing of sugar—then a key ingredient in Coca-Cola—put a damper on production during World War I. However, the drink's postwar popularity prompted a move to even larger facilities in 1929. Demand increased again in the 1930s, when the invention of electric ice coolers and coin-operated vending machines made Coca-Cola more accessible to consumers.

During World War II, Coca-Cola was again in short supply, and long lines formed at stores hours before Coca-Cola shipments arrived. To meet the demand, Houston Coca-Cola Bottling Company relocated in 1950 to its present home in Bissonnet, Texas—which, at that time, was the world's most modern bottling facility.

The Houston facility introduced and became the first company to market Sprite. Through the 1950s and 1960s, its product line expanded further to include Tab, Fresca, Mello Yello, diet Coke, Cherry Coke, and Minute Maid products. In 1977, the bottler also began producing soft drinks other than those of the Coca-Cola Company, including Welch's Grape and Strawberry drinks, Barq's Root Beer, Sunkist Orange, and White Rock and Schweppes mixers. Today, the Houston Coca-Cola Bottling Company employs more than 2,100 people at its main plant and offices, 12 sales warehouses, and canning plant.

"We have a loyal following in this city," reports David French, division vice president and general manager. "In response to that loyalty, we're active in and supportive of numerous community causes. We're continuing the tradition of quality products, services, and corporate citizenship that has become synonymous with Houston Coca-Cola Bottling Company."

The Houston Coca-Cola Bottling Company employs more than 2,100 people at its main plant and offices, 12 sales warehouses, and canning plant.

Small establishments like Mark Knox Flowers, as well as major corporations such as Continental Airlines, benefit from the services provided by the Texas Association of Business & Chambers of Commerce (TABCC). This association meets the needs of a diverse clientele with a clear focus on promoting a healthy business climate for all Texans. ● The blueprint for thriving economic development was created in 1922 by three San Antonio businessmen who founded the Texas State Manufacturers Association, which later became the Texas Association of Business (TAB). The trio recognized the start of a new business era and felt the need for a coordinated effort to deal with public policy issues. In 1995, TAB merged with the Texas Chamber of Commerce, the umbrella organization for hundreds of local chambers, many with roots dating back to the 1920s. TABCC now has 5,000 corporate members and 200 chambers, which in turn have 140,000 businesses as members. The rich history and combined strength of the two organizations position TABCC to lead Texas employers through the challenges and opportunities of a new millennium.

TABCC today is based in Austin with seven regions and 32 chapters statewide. The Southeast Texas Regional office is located in Houston and includes the Houston Coastal Chapter and Golden Triangle Chapter.

Working to Provide Information

The menu of TABCC membership benefits is stellar, starting with the association's promise to represent the interests of employers before the Texas Legislature and state regulatory agencies. "Information is vital to success," says Susan Tallas, regional vice president of the Southeast Texas Area. "With an average of 5,000 bills filed each session, you can be sure there will be legislation that businesses won't like. It may be in the form of a small amendment or even one word change. If it's legislation that will hurt business, we will work to eliminate it. We are the watchdog of business."

TABCC's Governmental Affairs team works on priority legislative issues such as economic development, environmental quality, health care, international trade, and taxes. TABCC's lobbying efforts have helped pass electric utility restructuring, franchise tax relief, and workers' compensation reform.

Members are kept informed about legislative and other business issues through a monthly newsletter, an overnight fax network, and a Web site located at www.tabcc.org. "We also make sure our members are well informed about elections," Tallas says. "We publish a book during campaign years that highlights who the candidates are and how they stand on issues important to Texas business."

Improving Employment Relations

Another important concern for TABCC members is employment relations. Small employers and human resource professionals can call the toll-free Employment Relations Hotline for advice on workplace situations, policies, laws, and regulations. The association also sponsors an annual Employment Relations Symposium, along with local workshops to explore human resource and labor law topics. TABCC members can also take advantage of money-saving group insurance and benefit packages for employers of all sizes.

The Southeast Region meets every other month and hosts key speakers from regulatory agencies, as well as legislators from Austin and from Washington, D.C.

"A vital economic climate is essential for the creation of jobs and expanded opportunity," Tallas says. "We invite Texas business leaders to join us in a partnership to benefit our state, as well as their businesses and employees."

The Texas Association of Business & Chambers of Commerce has been working for business across the Lone Star State for more than 75 years.

Stewart & Stevenson

Forming their original partnership in downtown Houston in 1902, C. Jim Stewart and Joe R. Stevenson each invested approximately $300 toward their entrepreneurial goal. Together, C. Jim Stewart & Stevenson blacksmith and carriage maker established Houston's first carriage repair and farrier. In doing so, they laid the foundation for a lifelong business philosophy that has carried the company through almost a century of business—a philosophy of diversification and hard work. ● From its inception, Stewart & Stevenson has evolved into a world leader in both the manufacturing and distribution of power related equipment. A commitment to service, innovative engineering, fair dealing, business integrity, and generations of dedicated employees has earned the company a strong positive reputation. Stewart & Stevenson today is a billion-dollar company which provides an array of products and services to a worldwide customer base.

Quality Service: The Roots of the Company

The leap from horseshoes to horsepower began in 1905, when the company restored a badly burned "Dixie Flyer" automobile. In 1938, the company entered the diesel engine business by securing the first General Motors diesel distributorship. This new distributorship gave Stewart & Stevenson the ability to begin an era of diversification by applying its diesel power. World War II brought with it a demand for diesel-driven equipment, and the company supplied mobile diesel generator sets, rebuilt Army jeep bodies and engines, and General Sherman tank engines. After the war ended, the company turned its manufacturing effort to items that included generator sets and equipment for the petroleum and aircraft ground support equipment industries. "Like any other company, we've had our ups and downs over the years, but because of our diversified products and services, we've been able to survive the many market fluctuations in the different industries in which we operate," says C. Jim Stewart III, vice president of marketing and public affairs.

The company's slogan of Service Anytime, Anywhere is the business philosophy that has guided the company through its growth worldwide. "Our service technicians and parts support are available to our customers on a

Beginning as a carriage repair shop and farrier, Stewart & Stevenson today produces a wide range of products, and is a leader in the manufacture of aircraft ground support equipment.

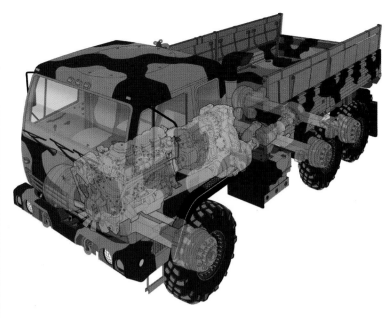

24-hours-a-day, 365-days-a-year basis. That's our guarantee," says Stewart.

From Horseshoes to Horsepower

Today, the company is divided into three major business segments: Engineered Power Systems Division, Power Products Division, and Tactical Vehicle Systems Division. The Engineered Power Systems Division provides a diverse selection of manufactured equipment, including well servicing and well stimulation equipment for the petroleum industry. Aircraft tow tractors, baggage tractors, air start units, and belt loaders are a few of the products manufactured by the company for the airline ground support equipment industry. The division's Rail King, a mobile railcar mover, provides simple, cost-effective switching operations for the railroad industry.

The Power Products Division is one of the largest distributors of diesel engines, as well as a manufacturer utilizing the Detroit Diesel, Electro-Motive, Deutz, and Waukesha lines of diesel engines. The company also distributes Thermo King refrigeration units; rental generators and air compressors; marine propulsion systems; material handling equipment; snow-removal equipment; and PowerLift, a system to help meet the mobility needs of the physically challenged.

The Tactical Vehicle Systems Division manufactures a state-of-the-art family of medium tactical vehicles for the U.S. Army. These vehicles were tested by the military and have met or exceeded their expectations and requirements. Stewart & Stevenson assembles the trucks at an assembly plant utilizing the latest in engineering and truck manufacturing techniques. This truck offers the U.S. military the most efficient and reliable truck in the world today.

"One of our hallmarks has been our 'can-do' attitude," Stewart says. "Over the years, we've had many people say, 'that can't be done,' and through the innovation of our employees, we've shown them that it can be done. That attitude, coupled with superior product engineering and design, has earned the company numerous design awards over the years throughout the industries we serve."

A Company Built on Generations

The company remains grounded in its belief that its almost 4,500 employees are its greatest asset. It is proud to highlight the generations of families that have worked with the company over the years, and continues successful internal programs such as profit sharing and an open-door management policy.

"We have grown into a large company, but we still know we could never have built the company into such a successful business without the loyalty, perseverance, and dedication of our employees," Stewart says. "Employees at Stewart & Stevenson feel they have a stake in the company's success."

Stewart & Stevenson employees are encouraged to take active roles in community events. The company sponsors and participates in many educational programs including scholarships, mentoring, and adopt-a-school programs. Employees volunteer to take part in civic events like the Houston Livestock and Rodeo Show, the Montgomery County Fair scholarship programs, the March of Dimes, Walk America, the Arthritis Foundation, and United Way.

"We are proud to call Houston our home because this city provides such a fertile ground for growth," Stewart says. "We're thankful to the community for being so supportive of us, and we are proud to give back whenever we can."

This coiled tubing system—including injection head—is typical of the oilfield equipment manufactured by the Petroleum Products Division(left).

Stewart & Stevenson produces the FMTV-A1 for the U.S. Army (right).

Stewart & Stevenson's power rental system is available 24 hours a day, seven days a week.

Halliburton Company

The name Halliburton means many things to many people. For most Texans, it conjures images of oil exploration and production, an industry the Halliburton Company has led with innovative services for the past 90 years. For Houstonians, Brown & Root, Halliburton's engineering and construction division, is the name behind many of the city's roadways and landmarks. Otherwise, the Halliburton name may bring to mind one of numerous firms that have merged into the company over the years, from Landmark Graphics' innovative oil and gas exploration software to Dresser Equipment Group's leading equipment manufacturing divisions.

No matter what people may think of when they hear the name, today's Halliburton is creating a vivid image as a worldwide industry leader and global solutions provider for energy services, engineering, construction and maintenance services, and energy equipment.

A History of Growth

In 1919, brothers George and Herman Brown and their brother-in-law Dan Root formed an engineering and construction company in Houston, and landed several road construction projects across Texas. Following Herman's death in 1962, George Brown approached an oil and gas service company founded by entrepreneur Erle P. Halliburton. Halliburton had started a well-cementing business in 1919 from his one-room home in Oklahoma, and by the early 1960s, he had expanded to 201 offices in 22 states and nearly 20 foreign countries.

According to Brown, "We began to look around for a service company that we thought had the same concept for opera-

tion and treatment of employees and free enterprise that we had." The combination of Halliburton with Brown & Root began a series of strategic mergers and acquisitions that over the past 30 years has created a $17 billion, global company. Halliburton is now one of Houston's largest private-sector employers, with more than 17,500 Houstonians and another 17,000 area sub-contractor employees working on a variety of energy, engineering, and construction projects for customers around the world. In fact, with just under 100,000 employees and 750 offices in 130 countries, Halliburton is one of the few companies with operations on each of the seven continents.

The 1998 merger between the Halliburton Company and Dresser Industries, a leading global supplier of energy-related products and services, created the largest oil-field services company in the world, with annual revenues exceeding its closest competitor by about 50 percent.

Innovative Leadership

Halliburton boasts a track record for innovation, whether creating new products, such as Real Time Reservoir Solutions™, which helps monitor remote oil exploration jobs on a real-time basis, or designing business practices, such as partnering with customers on oil and gas and major engineering projects.

"Our customers know that not only do we provide a wide array of equipment, services, and technology, we're experts in providing innovative solutions to their toughest challenges, particularly for deep-water drilling in difficult environments,"

From top:

Erle P. Halliburton is the founder of the company that is today Halliburton Company.

Headquartered in Houston, Halliburton's Landmark Graphics Corporation is the leading supplier of open, integrated information systems and professional services to the upstream exploration and production industry.

The Exxon Chemical Plant in Baytown, Texas, was engineered and constructed by Halliburton's Kellogg Brown & Root.

notes Dave Lesar, chairman, president, and chief executive officer. "Customers come to us for leading-edge, value-added solutions. A high standard of excellence is evident in everything we do."

Each Halliburton division is charged with developing new products and services that capitalize on new technologies and maintain the company's leadership in the industry. Meeting the needs of its marketplace is easy for the company because of its flat organizational structure. "We have very few layers of management, which enables us to process information, analyze situations, and make decisions quickly," says Lesar.

"In the 1990s alone," he adds, "Halliburton received more than 4,000 patents and industry awards for its contributions to the energy and engineering industries. We produce more technology and patents than anyone else in the oilfield service industry."

Halliburton's use of information technology is helping the company maintain its leadership. "The bottom line is that Halliburton has a great legacy of innovation, service, and quality. In the same way as when the company was formed, we're changing very quickly. We have to be as agile now as we were as a start-up company. Web technology will enable us to do that and we expect E-commerce to play a major role in the way the company presents itself to employees, suppliers, and customers," Lesar says.

Halliburton Today

Halliburton today consists of three major business segments: the Energy Service Group, Engineering and Construction Group, and Dresser Equipment Group.

The Energy Service Group offers the broadest array of products and services to upstream oil and gas customers worldwide, stretching from the manufacturing of drill bits and other downhole tools to the

engineering and fabrication of offshore platforms and field processing equipment. This group is comprised of three business units: Halliburton Energy Services, Landmark Graphics Corporation, and Brown & Root Energy Services.

Halliburton Energy Services provides services for oil and gas exploration, development, and production, ranging from initial evaluation of producing formations to drilling, completion, production

On a worldwide basis, Landmark Graphics and Halliburton Energy Services experts work closely with their customers to help maximize understanding of their reservoir assets.

The 504-foot high Bhumiphol Dam was constructed by Brown & Root in 1962.

enhancement, and well maintenance for a single well or an entire field.

Landmark Graphics Corporation supplies exploration and production information systems, software, and services to help energy companies worldwide locate and manage reservoirs.

Brown & Root Energy Services supplies engineering and construction services to the upstream oil and gas industry, including the fabrication and operation of facilities needed for production and transportation of oil and gas.

Backed with engineering excellence and construction experience, the Engineering and Construction Group is able to take on end-to-end projects of any size in the world, from design and project management to construction and maintenance. It is made up of Kellogg Brown & Root (KBR) and Brown & Root Services.

Kellogg Brown & Root combines two of the most widely recognized names in the engineering and construction industry—the M.W. Kellogg Company and Halliburton's Brown & Root. The new KBR provides project development, technology licensing and development, consulting, project management, engineering/procurement/construction, and operations and maintenance services.

Brown & Root Services is a leading nonenergy, government, and private sector services provider of engineering, architecture, construction, management, logistics, and advanced technology.

The Dresser Equipment Group designs and manufactures a wide variety of sophisticated equipment used primarily in the energy, refining, and petrochemical industries, including valves and other flow control devices, measurement instruments, power systems, compressors, and pumps.

The Dresser Equipment Group includes the Dresser Manufacturing Division (DMD), a leading worldwide supplier of high-performance rotary gas meters to the natural gas industry. Dresser Instrument manufactures pressure and temperature indication and control devices. DMD Roots ranks as the world leader in manufacturing and repair of rotary equipment.

Dresser Valve Division leads in the manufacture of valves, while Dresser Waukesha produces spark-ignited, gas-fueled engines widely used in field compression applications and packaged engine-generator sets for stationary industrial applications. Dresser Wayne is a maker of automation control and fuel dispensing systems.

Outstanding Accomplishments

When the resources and talents of some of the world's best companies are combined, great things happen—and over the years, Halliburton has achieved quite a few milestones in the industries it serves.

For example, during the late 1960s, Halliburton's innovative Hydrofrac process had added more than 8 billion barrels of oil to North American reserves since the introduction of the process. Brown & Root-Northrup received the Medal of Freedom for devising the ingenious makeshift carbon dioxide removal system that helped rescue the Apollo 13 astronauts. And following Operation Desert Storm in Kuwait, Halliburton crews helped bring 320 burning wells under control. Brown & Root was also selected to assess and repair damaged public buildings in Kuwait, winning a contract from the U.S. Army for worldwide logistics support planning.

Clockwise from top:
Houstonians George (left) and Herman Brown, together with brother-in-law Dan Root founded Brown & Root in 1919. The company was acquired by Halliburton in 1962, and seven years later was the largest engineering and construction firm in the United States.

The Total Abandonment Services alliance (TAS) combines the efforts of Halliburton Energy Services and Global Industries in projects such as the removing of this massive structure.

The visualization room of Halliburton's Reservoir Decision Center in Houston enables customers and Halliburton team members to collaborate on multiple projects at one time.

Houston's new ballpark and home to the Houston Astros, Enron Field, was constructed by Halliburton's Brown & Root Services.

Halliburton's Brown & Root Energy Services has designed and built oil and gas production and transportation facilities in every corner of the world, from distant and demanding fields in the North Sea, Europe, Africa, Asia, and Australia to the promising deep waters of the Gulf of Mexico.

Halliburton employees literally helped build Houston in the 20th century, from landmarks such as the 70,000-seat Rice Stadium to the Ship Channel bridge. Today, they are still at work building Houston, with projects like the new Enron Field baseball stadium, which features a retractable roof, and NASA's Johnson Space Center, where Brown & Root Services provides engineering support for both the Space Shuttle and International Space Station programs.

In addition to the company's physical legacy of buildings and major roadways in the city, Halliburton employees have created a tradition of improving the quality of life in the Houston area. Each year, em-

ployees volunteer and support a variety of programs in the area, including the March of Dimes, Juvenile Diabetes Foundation, Houston International Festival, Junior Achievement, and others. Many of the leaders who helped build Halliburton into a prominent international enterprise also played key roles in molding Houston into a world-class city.

The future looks promising for this worldwide industry leader. "Like any company, we're always looking for new opportunities to succeed," says Lesar. "We're continuing to grow—not for the sake of getting bigger, but to become more profitable. We will continue to provide fully integrated packages of solutions and services to our valued customers."

3-D visualization and integrated wellbore planning tools enable Landmark customers to design optimum wellbore trajectories through complex reservoir systems (left).

Halliburton's Brown & Root Services is involved in a joint-venture contract to provide comprehensive base operating support services at the Johnson Space Center (right).

In 1935, the United States was in the midst of one of the most devastating periods in its history, the Great Depression. Consumer confidence was at an all-time low, and depositors were suspicious of the stability of financial institutions. It was during this same year that 196 employees of Shell Oil Company pooled their financial resources in the total amount of $980 and formed the Shell Employees Federal Credit Union (SEFCU). These founding members sought to create a nonprofit financial cooperative in which they would each own shares. Members were limited to a $200 maximum deposit and a $50 maximum loan amount.

A lot has changed since the 1930s. With seven locations in the Houston area, SEFCU has grown to more than 25,000 members with assets in excess of $160 million. As one of Houston's top 10 credit unions, its menu of services includes a variety of deposit accounts, loan products, and services. Each account is insured up to $100,000 by the National Credit Union Administration (NCUA).

Many things, however, have stayed the same. The credit union is still a member-owned and -driven financial cooperative where people are worth more than money. With the original grassroots ideal still intact, SEFCU's mission continues to focus on servicing and satisfying members' changing financial needs, and on becoming their lifetime financial partner.

With the opening of its new service center in downtown Houston at One Shell Plaza, Shell Employees Federal Credit Union (SEFCU) has created the prototype for 21st-century financial institutions.

Innovative Products and Services

One of the tools SEFCU utilizes in accommodating changing member needs is the Dream Builders accounts package, which includes accounts such as Spreading Your Wings, Taking Flight, Reaching for the Sky, and Safe Landing. SEFCU has designed each account as a compilation of products and services geared toward assisting its members at different life stages.

"Our goal is to represent all generations, from Generation Xers to baby boomers to World War II veterans. The financial needs of a college student are very different from the needs of someone who has been out in the business world for 25 years," says Andy Martingano, vice president of marketing and business development. "Free checking and preapproval on a car loan might be among the top priorities for a college student, whereas a financial investment review and a pre-approved home improvement loan could be very helpful for the business professional."

To stay in touch with the financial needs of its members, SEFCU utilizes technology to track membership demographics, and uses this statistical data to target member needs.

SEFCU also remains sensitive to changes in the economy. "It used to be that people worked for one company during their entire career. Now, it's common for a person to work for a variety of companies, and with downsizing, mergers, and industry fluctuations, we want to be responsive to our members' changing financial needs," Martingano says.

SEFCU is committed to the credit union philosophy of "once a member, always a member." "We're not following the job, we're following the person," Martingano says. Membership is extended to an employee's immediate family as well. "All family members are welcome to share in the benefits of credit union membership," he says.

Education is an important element in rendering a personalized level of service for members. SEFCU's educational seminars cover topics that range from financial planning and investments to how best to finance a car. "Education is the hallmark of credit unions. A more educated member is more likely to make sound financial decisions," Martingano says.

SEFCU's Service Partner Program offers a number of complementary services, including insurance, financial planning products, and travel services, as well as cellular phones and pagers.

As a member-owned, nonprofit cooperative, SEFCU invites members to share in its ownership through a savings account with a low monthly minimum balance and no monthly service fee. Dividends are paid quarterly, and a board of directors, elected by members, governs the credit union's business activities.

An Eye toward the Future

With advances in technology, SEFCU has expanded its product and service menu, offering such amenities as automated lending, telephone transactions, and ATMs. "We have a very savvy membership base and lifestyles have changed through the years.

One member may embrace home banking, while another member may still want face-to-face contact with our relationship coordinators," Martingano says. "We pride ourselves on embracing technological advances while maintaining that personal touch, which distinguishes us from more traditional financial institutions."

With the opening of its new downtown service center, SEFCU has created the prototype for 21st-century financial institutions. The facility is located in the tunnel system of Houston's central business district beneath One Shell Plaza, and features amenities such as on-line access to member accounts via several in-house computers; two fully staffed kiosks, dedicated to providing members with complete financial services; a special services area, which includes mortgage lending, Lincoln Financial Advisors investment services, and auto leasing; and four TV monitors located throughout the center, which deliver the latest financial, sports, and entertainment news.

SEFCU is positioning itself for the future by closely tracking member relationships and monitoring the changing financial needs of its members, especially during its year-long 65th anniversary celebration. It will add virtual branching and E-commerce services, and is looking toward co-oping its services with regional and national credit unions. Says Martingano, "What sets us apart from traditional financial institutions is the fact that we remain member owned and member driven. The changes we make in the future will be closely aligned with the changing financial needs of our members."

In addition to its downtown service center at One Shell Plaza (top left and right), SEFCU has facilities located throughout the Houston area, including executive offices at Two Shell Plaza (bottom right) and its southwest service center (bottom left).

The Pepsi Bottling Group of Houston

From the first 8-ounce glass bottle with what is now vintage Pepsi labeling to a convenient, 20-ounce plastic bottle designed to fit perfectly in automobile cupholders, Pepsi has undergone significant changes in its more than 100 years of marketing. ● Developed in 1898 as a cure for indigestion, the original Pepsi product has evolved into a $10 billion worldwide enterprise with a diverse family of products. The Pepsi Bottling Group, based in Somers, New York, is the world's largest Pepsi bottler, with more than 40,000 employees around the world.

A Taste for Life

Houston's love for Pepsi products began more than 60 years ago. Carl Lockshin and brothers Joe, Julius, and N. H. Darsky founded Pepsi-Cola Bottling Co. of Houston and began bottling and distributing the famous beverage in 1939. In 1951, Golden Age Beverage Company won the parent company's bottling appointment and opened its first local plant in 1955.

The franchise returned to Pepsi-Cola Bottling Co. of Houston in 1963. In 1967, George and Fred Pothoff of Union Bottling Works bought the franchise from Lockshin and his brothers. The Pothoffs built the company's current headquarters on LaPorte Freeway; the grand opening was attended by film star Joan Crawford, who was married at the time to the PepsiCo chairman.

In 1970, PepsiCo took control of the operation, and 10 years later, added another plant to the Houston operation with the purchase of Conroe Packaging Inc. Since then, the Houston territory has expanded with the addition of the Beaumont; Lake Charles, Louisiana; and Bryan/College Station service areas.

Today, the Pepsi Bottling Group of Houston, as the organization is now known, serves more than 18,000 customers and provides service to most of southeast Texas and parts of Louisiana. With more than 600 employees, the company operates two plants and produces approximately 30 million cases of products annually. The 135,000-square-foot Houston facility produces bottled packages and fountain soft drinks, while the Conroe plant only produces canned products.

Over the years, the family of Pepsi products has grown significantly, and the company now produces 150 different beverages, including Pepsi, Diet Pepsi, PepsiOne, Mountain Dew, Lipton Brisk, Aquafina bottled water, and Frappuccino, a coffee drink produced in partnership with Starbucks Coffee Company.

A Generation Ahead

The Pepsi Bottling Group of Houston stays active in charitable organizations. Its sponsorships include the annual March of Dimes Walk America event, the Children's Festival, and the MS 150 Bike Tour, which raises funds for the National Multiple Sclerosis Society. In addition, many of the company's employees volunteer in a wide array of community programs.

"The Houston community has been very supportive of our operations over the years," says Chris Van Horn, general manager of the Houston Market Unit for the Pepsi Bottling Group of Houston. "Wanting to give back to the community is only natural."

The Pepsi Bottling Group of Houston produces a wide variety of Pepsi products.

The Greater Southwest Houston Chamber of Commerce has been helping its members achieve success for more than 50 years. Along the way, the communities served by the chamber have flourished, creating some of Houston's most desirable locales in which to live and work. ● Founded in 1949 as the Bellaire Chamber of Commerce, the organization soon began connecting with neighboring areas. Today, Bellaire is one of three cities and nine Houston communities served by the chamber. The others include Astrodome/South Loop, Braeswood/Stella Link, Fondren Southwest, Greenway Plaza, Gulfton, Meyerland/South Post Oak, Sharpstown, City of Southside Place, Rice Village/Texas Medical Center, Westbury, and the City of West University Place. This large geographic area has a culturally diverse population of 260,000 people.

Chamber President and CEO Trish Wise says the residents and businesses in this area enjoy three major benefits: "People are attracted to this area because of the friendly atmosphere, the close proximity to downtown Houston and The Texas Medical Center, and the top-quality public and private schools.

"The majority of the chamber's 600-plus members are owner-operated," Wise adds. "We offer a full buffet of services for small businesses." Among the offerings, the University of Houston Small Business Development Center sets up one day a week at the chamber to offer free assistance. The Service Corps of Retired Executives (SCORE) also lends its expertise. Between workshops, networking events, seminars, community festivals, and other meetings, chamber members can choose from a menu of about 60 activities a month.

Area Highlights

The area promotes the kind of friendly atmosphere where a small business can thrive alongside medical industry giants. The chamber's service area is home to some of Houston's largest hospitals, including those at The Texas Medical Center, along with Memorial Hermann Hospital Southwest, Bayou City Medical Center, and Bellaire Medical Center.

Greenway Plaza is a hot spot for business and urban living, with gleaming office towers, high-rise condos, sports at the Compaq Center, and many of the city's top restaurants and clubs. New development is big—at least two exclusive apartment complexes, two hotel properties, a 24-screen theater, an assisted living center, and four major retail shopping centers are going up in the area.

The Astros have moved out of the expansive Astrodome to a downtown stadium, and business leaders are excited about the new potential of the Astrodomain as a convention center.

More than 59,000 jobs are tied to the Rice Village area, with many of those at The Texas Medical Center's 42 non-profit institutions. Majestic oaks line the streets near prestigious Rice University, the museum district, and Hermann Park. Wedged between Rice University and West University Place is The Village, one of Houston's first shopping districts. Shoppers also delight in the stores of Houston's first air-conditioned mall, Sharpstown Center, and the newly renovated Meyerland Plaza.

The area also offers a variety of residential options—from apartments and high-rise condos to middle-class, single-family homes and mansions to assisted living centers. "While the options are diverse, the neighborhoods all have one thing in common—strong civic pride," Wise says. "Many of the areas have spearheaded initiatives that have revitalized the economy and improved the quality of life."

Clockwise from top:
Welcoming new members with ribbon cuttings is a fun and frequent activity of the Greater Southwest Houston Chamber of Commerce.

The chamber is proud to own its building on Rice Avenue in Bellaire, Texas.

On August 12, 1999, hundreds of chamber members celebrated 50 years of the chamber Connecting Commerce & Community.

▲ TRISH STRANGMEYER PHOTOGRAPHY

The University of Texas M. D. Anderson Cancer Center

Making cancer history is both a statement of accomplishment and a goal for The University of Texas M. D. Anderson Cancer Center. One of several health care giants in Houston's renowned Texas Medical Center, M. D. Anderson has contributed major advances in cancer medicine for more than half a century. When the Texas Legislature created the Texas State Cancer Hospital and Division of Cancer Research in 1941, the prospect of curing cancer was bleak, but research hopes were high for controlling the disease. In 1942, the institution's name was changed to M. D. Anderson Hospital for Cancer Research of The University of Texas in recognition of

Clockwise from top:
Bruno Fornage, M.D., performs an ultrasound at The University of Texas M. D. Anderson Cancer Center for a breast cancer patient.

Cancer risk factors are explained to a patient by Theresa B. Bevers, M.D.

The Albert B. and Margaret M. Alkek Hospital was built to meet future cancer needs.

the philanthropy of Monroe Dunaway Anderson, whose foundation donated an interim site and land for permanent facilities in Houston. Today, The University of Texas M. D. Anderson Cancer Center is one of the world's most respected and productive centers devoted exclusively to cancer patient care, research, education, and prevention.

"Approximately 60 percent of Americans affected by cancer now can be cured, and an increasing number of others will have prolonged and improved quality of life," says John Mendelsohn, M.D., president. "As we enter the 21st century, I am confident that our faculty and staff will continue making cancer history for as long as this complex disease challenges us."

From Lab to Patient Care

M. D. Anderson's greatest strength lies in its ability to translate scientific knowledge gained in the laboratory to more effective therapies for common as well as rare forms of cancer. Teams of scientists, physicians, and support staff routinely collaborate in developing better ways to diagnose, treat, and prevent cancer.

At any one time, about 600 clinical trials are being conducted to assess new approaches for surgery, chemotherapy, radiation therapy, and biological therapy. Many therapies have become the standard for community care after being evaluated at M. D. Anderson and other leading cancer centers. Through clinical trials, improved and less invasive surgical techniques have been developed for breast, head and neck, and bone cancers, among others. Surgery often is combined with at least one other treatment modality.

Among early clinical advances at M. D. Anderson were the design and testing of the first cobalt-60 unit and introduction of other powerful radiation therapy equip-

ment and treatment techniques. Numerous anticancer drugs and biologic agents have been proven effective through clinical research. Ongoing studies are demonstrating the role of gene therapy to replace or correct faulty genes associated with lung, head and neck, prostate, and other cancer sites.

M. D. Anderson has broadened research in epidemiology and behavioral science to strengthen the field of cancer prevention. Research continues showing that chemoprevention agents can reverse premalignant lesions and prevent second primary head and neck cancers as well as breast and lung cancers in individuals at high risk for those tumors. The array of prevention services ranges from personalized risk assessment to genetic counseling.

One of the Best

U.S. News & World Report and other consumer publications consistently rank M. D. Anderson as one of the best centers for cancer care. It was one of the first three Comprehensive Cancer Centers created by the National Cancer Act of 1971, and, today, is among 36 such institutions designated by the National Cancer Institute. M. D. Anderson holds the highest level of accreditation from the Joint Commission on Accreditation of Healthcare Organizations.

The multidisciplinary approach to cancer care was pioneered at M. D. Anderson. Teams of physicians and other health professionals work together in dedicated care centers to coordinate each patient's continuum of services. The research program also involves interdisciplinary collaboration among scientists and physicians. Last year, the institution received the highest number of research grants of any academic center from both the National Cancer Institute and the American Cancer Society.

The Art of Healing

Along with the science of treating cancer, M. D. Anderson has introduced innovative programs that incorporate rehabilitation, pain control, and emotional help for patients touched by cancer.

Through the Place … of Wellness, patients can access services that focus on the whole person. It is the first on-campus facility at a comprehensive cancer center with programs to help both patients and their loved ones adjust to living with and recovering from cancer. Activities include nutrition classes, yoga, tai chi, guided imagery, support groups, and art, music, and humor sessions.

Cancer care available at M. D. Anderson attracts patients from throughout the world. Almost 42 percent of patients come from outside Texas. The International Patient

Center provides a multilingual staff to assist patients and families from other countries. Diverse support services are offered to patients and families staying at the Jesse H. Jones Rotary House International, a 198-room hotel located across the street.

Growing for the Future

While improving the spectrum of cancer care, M. D. Anderson has expanded its physical plant to meet increasing service demands. With the opening in 1998 of the Clinical Research Building and the Albert B. and Margaret M. Alkek Hospital, the total size of M. D. Anderson's facilities in the Texas Medical Center reached 4.4 million square feet. An ongoing building program includes adding

a new Basic Science Research Building for collaborative projects among Texas Medical Center institutions.

M. D. Anderson also operates a Science Park in Bastrop County near Austin, Texas. One unit is devoted to research focusing on the environmental causes of cancer, and the second unit provides specialized veterinary services and animal models for many institutions to conduct biomedical research.

A substantial amount of M. D. Anderson's physical and program growth has been possible through support from individuals, foundations, and corporations. "The steadily increasing—and greatly appreciated—private philanthropy provides an extra edge in our determination to conquer cancer," Mendelsohn says.

Clockwise from top:
Subrata Sen, Ph.D. (left), and Dihua Yu, M.D., Ph.D., conduct collaborative molecular research.

Janet Price, Ph.D. (left), trains graduate student Emily Van Laar in a cancer biology laboratory.

Nurse Vivian Dorsey monitors outpatient chemotherapy for Christopher Hoeft.

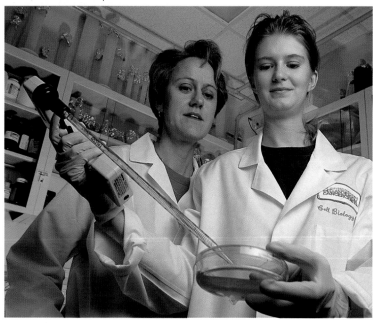

The future has never looked brighter for Texas Southern University (TSU). With plans to lead the way in 21st-century technological training, and with new relationships in the Houston-area business industry, student enrollment figures and community pride are soaring. "I envision Texas Southern University in the 21st century as an independent institution of higher learning of the first class," says TSU President Priscilla D. Slade, who has been credited with bringing the university into a progressive new arena. ● Slade's Vision 2000 Plan contains five focal points, which include fiscal responsibility, academic and faculty excellence, service and accountability in administration, a hospitable learning and living environment, and a commitment to community outreach.

Globally Recognized Academic Programs

Since 1947, programs at the university have interfaced with the processes for identifying and resolving urban problems. Programs have also emerged along traditional lines, resulting in the present configuration of seven colleges and schools: the College of Arts and Sciences, the College of Pharmacy and Health Sciences, the School of Technology, the College of Education, the Thurgood Marshall School of Law, the Jesse H. Jones School of Business, and the Graduate School. Other areas of emphasis are underscored in the university's various research centers, the Weekend College and Division of Continuing Education, the General University Academic Center, and the Frederick Douglass Honors Institute.

In pursuit of its mission, TSU offers programs and instruction of the highest quality leading to baccalaureate, master's, professional, and doctoral degrees; provides academic and non-academic areas with services designed to facilitate the total development of individual students; fosters quality research accompanied by a strong faculty, state-of-the-art facilities, and superior learning opportunities for students; utilizes its resources to make the urban environs more habitable by improving the delivery of social services and applying knowledge and technology to pressing social and economic problems; and provides a conducive environment for a substantial number of minorities—especially African-Americans—to develop a full awareness and appreciation of their ethnic and cultural heritage.

TSU emphasizes many of the disciplines that are essential to public institutions—education, public works, criminal justice, social work, communications, technology, and more. TSU graduates represent more than 34 percent of the teachers and administrators in the Houston Independent School District. Fifty percent of the African-American and 20 percent of the Mexican-American law graduates in Texas earned their law degrees from TSU's Thurgood Marshall School of Law. In addition, more than 80 percent of students from the College of Pharmacy and Health Sciences pass their certifications the first time, representing one of the highest certification ratios in the country.

TSU has a multiethnic faculty, 70 percent of which holds doctoral degrees. "The staff works diligently to guarantee that students learn what they need to know," Slade says, "not only about the fields of study they embrace, but also about how to advance their opportunities to realize their dreams."

The university receives about $7 million a year of outside support for research. The primary areas of funding are health sciences, environmental science, space science, transportation, alternative energy technologies, superconductivity, and computer science. TSU has developed specialties in environmental science and environmental toxicology,

With an eye on the future, Texas Southern University (TSU) is set to add to its distinguished alumni roster by graduating students with the training and skills needed to lead the way through the 21st century.

solar power, and diseases affecting minorities. The school's expertise led to the formation of a Ph.D. program in environmental toxicology at TSU, the only graduate program in this field in the Houston area.

Distinguished Graduates

Distinguished TSU graduates include such past and present political leaders as the late U.S. Congressman Mickey Leland, the late U.S. Congresswoman Barbara Jordan, and State Senator Rodney Ellis. Internationally renowned jazz musician Kirk Whalum graduated from TSU, as did Valeria Horton-Dickson, who represents the United States in foreign affairs; Michael Strahan, defensive tackle for the New York Giants; and Tony Wyllie, who leads the media relations office for the Houston Texans.

TSU graduates leading the way in Houston include A. Martin Wickliff, partner, Wickliff & Hall, PC; Gerald Smith, president and CEO of Smith Graham & Company, the largest privately owned minority investment company in the nation; Jackie Martin, president of United Way of Texas Gulf Coast; Clarence Bradford, Houston chief of police; David Whatley, director of administration for the Veteran's Hospital; Christopher Oliver, president of Houston Community College Board of Trustees; Alvia Wardlaw, the first African-American curator in the state of Texas; Leslie Mays, COO of diversity for Shell Oil Company; El Franco Lee, Harris County commissioner; Milton Carroll, president and CEO of Instrument Products; Anthony Hall, City of Houston attorney; Pluria Marshall,

founder and executive director of the National Black Media Coalition; and John Crump, executive director of the National Bar Association.

With an eye on the future, TSU is set to add to this distinguished alumni roster by graduating students with the training and skills needed to lead the way through the 21st century.

Training Tomorrow's Leaders

While most of TSU's 7,000 undergraduate and graduate students are native Texans, the diverse TSU student body offers a unique experience unmatched by most institutions

of higher education. Students from Nigeria, Asia, China, Central America, Mexico, Puerto Rico, the West Indies, and Canada, as well as students from the United States, can feel at home in the university's nurturing environment.

"Our primary reason for existing is for students to be able to see themselves as the future leaders of Houston and the world," Slade says. "TSU is a special-purpose institution with an open-access policy, which means our doors are open just as wide for an average student as for an above-average student. The proud tradition that is Texas Southern University begins and ends with its students."

TSU proudly displays its motto: Excellence in Achievement.

The College of Pharmacy and Health Sciences is dedicated to providing quality education and leadership to its students.

University of St. Thomas

Nestled amid a historic, residential community and Houston's distinguished Museum District is one the Southwest's jewels: the University of St. Thomas (UST). ● Founded in 1947 by the Basilian Fathers, a community of priests, at the request of the bishop of the Galveston-Houston diocese, the institution is Houston's first and only Catholic university. The independent, coeducational, Catholic school places a strong emphasis on the liberal arts and, in its 50 years, has earned both regional and national reputations for the diversity of its student body and academic excellence. ● Since 1994, UST has received nine national accolades, including repeat citations for excellence from *U.S. News and World Report* and *Money Magazine*. Accredited by the Southern Association of Colleges and Schools, the university offers 29 undergraduate majors, including preprofessional programs in law, engineering, and medicine; several master's programs; and a doctoral program in philosophy. UST has an impressive 6 percent of its student body in study abroad programs. According to statistics published in the *Chronicle of Higher Education* on study-abroad programs, UST ranks third nationally, behind the University of Notre Dame and Duke University. Guided by Catholic traditions and heritage, the university welcomes students of all faiths and is committed to offering programs that meet the needs of the church and community.

Broad Liberal Arts Programs

UST's long-standing mission is twofold: intellectual and spiritual. Holding steadfast to the Basilian Fathers' motto, "Teach me goodness, discipline, and knowledge," UST officials believe reason and faith coexist, and they are dedicated to teaching and learning truth wherever it exists. The goal is to bring the light of faith to ideas that shape the world, and to cultivate the life of the mind and the spirit.

To do that, the university offers a broad and coherent undergraduate liberal arts core curriculum in philosophy, theology, the humanities, social sciences, mathematics, and science, with philosophy and theology classes providing an integrating framework for all undergraduate academic programs. Graduate programs include a master of business administration, master of science in information systems, master of science in accounting, master of international business, master of education, master in liberal arts, master of arts in philosophy, and doctor of philosophy. The Graduate School of Theology, the only such Catholic program in the Texas Gulf Coast region, offers a master of divinity, master of arts in theology, and a master of pastoral studies. While the university follows a semester system, with fall classes beginning in August and the spring semester commencing in January, UST also offers summer sessions, a compressed track, and an intersession program, which takes place during the break between the fall and spring semesters.

Diverse Enrollment, Esteemed Faculty

The University of St. Thomas opened its doors to 40 students in 1947, and in fall 1998 saw enrollment reach an all-time high of nearly 2,800. High-achieving students from across the country and around the globe are attracted to the university. Of the 1999 entering freshman class, 37 percent ranked in the top 10 percent of their high school classes, and the middle 50 percent of freshmen averaged between 1,070 and 1,240 on the SAT. While most of UST's students hail from the Lone Star State, students come from 23 states and 58 countries. In 1998-1999, African-Americans, Asian-Americans, Hispanics, and international students made up 45 percent of the university's student population.

UST's renowned faculty complements its diverse student body. Nearly 90 percent of the 200 full-time and part-time faculty members hold the highest degree in their fields of discipline. To allow professors ample one-on-one time with students, class

University of St. Thomas is located in the heart of Houston, near downtown and the city's historic Museum District. On campus, students gather on the steps of the Link Lee Mansion, which houses the University's administrative offices (top left). Students make time for learning and leisure at the John H. Crooker Center, the hub of student life activities (top right). The Chapel of St. Basil is the focal point of the Academic Mall, designed by famed architect Philip Johnson (bottom).

sizes are kept small, averaging 14 people. Professors participate in undergraduate research projects, campus organizations, and community service projects with students, while also providing a superior record of scholarly achievements.

The university's faculty has earned its reputation for distinction regionally and internationally. One of its distinguished members is Dr. Ronald Hatchett, director of the school's Center for International Studies and an expert on the Balkans. Hatchett was thrust into the international media spotlight during his involvement in the negotiations for the release of the American prisoners of war in Kosovo in 1999. A familiar face to Houstonians as world affairs analyst for a local television station, Hatchett was the first person to interview Yugoslavian President Slobodan Milosevic and was instrumental in keeping viewers updated on the Balkan crisis.

Campus Life

As the university becomes better known on the international scene for its faculty and its academic programs, its campus continues to evolve as well. UST's growing campus, located on Montrose Boulevard, is a serene complex of modern facilities and quaint, older houses, which were once homes to some of Houston's founders and leaders, including billionaire businessman Howard Hughes. On-campus housing for students includes a residence hall, university houses, and apartments.

The center of campus is the academic mall, where students mingle before and after classes and hold activities. Classrooms, faculty offices, a student center, and a gymnasium surround the academic quadrangle. Towering 70 feet above the quad is the striking architecture of the Chapel of St. Basil, which is dedicated to St. Basil the Great, a fourth-century bishop and patron of Chris-

tian educators. The chapel's striking architecture and unique design, which includes a grand 24-karat, gold-leaf dome topped with a seven-foot cross, draws frequent visitors from the community, and Mass is celebrated there four times daily.

Southwest's Premier Catholic Institution

As the university continues to grow—in physical size, student enrollment, and program offerings—it also continues to increase its commitment to academic excellence, social responsibility, and the highest ethical and religious values. In the next millennium, the university will respond to the challenges presented to its mission by poverty, globalization, limited economic resources, changing technology, and shifting population trends. As the premier Catholic university in the Southwest, UST will remain committed to its rich traditions and to the highest ideals of academic excellence, confidence in reason, social responsibility, and the life of faith.

Learning is enhanced in Robertson Hall's state-of-the-art chemistry lab (top left) and the Malloy Computer Lab (bottom left). Students meet for study sessions in the Guinan Hall lobby (top right). Afterwards, friends head outdoors enjoying Houston's dazzling summers and mild winters (bottom right).

Founded in 1955 through the joint efforts of Maestro Walter Herbert and cultural leader Mrs. Louis G. Lobit, Houston Grand Opera (HGO) had an inaugural season featuring two performances of two operas. Over the years, the organization has become internationally renowned for its unique, delicately balanced approach to programming. ● Today, with an annual budget of more than $20 million, it is the fifth-largest opera company in the United States and reaches 1.8 million people annually. HGO presents seven to 10 productions each season in three repertory periods. It has been under the acclaimed leadership of David Gockley, general director, since 1972, and recently added the talented Patrick Summers as music director.

"We want to share opera with audiences who have never before seen a performance," says Gockley. "We want people to see that opera is for everyone."

Creating an American Voice

HGO has debuted 25 world premieres and six American premieres, and has become known for the developing and nurturing of American artists and composers. Its imaginative presentations of masterpieces from the traditional operatic repertoire, coupled with its presentation of contemporary productions such as *Porgy and Bess, Treemonisha, Harvey Milk,* and *Jackie O,* have earned the opera its stellar reputation. HGO remains the only opera house in the world to have won a Tony, two Grammy awards, and two Emmy awards.

The year 1987 marked a major milestone in the company's history when the opera debuted its first three productions in its new residence, the Wortham Theater Center. The $72 million state-of-the-art facility houses both the 2,400-seat Brown and 1,100-seat Cullen theaters. The Wortham was constructed during one of the worst economic periods in the city's history and was funded entirely with private donations.

In addition to its commitment to staging productions from a traditional operatic repertoire, HGO commissions new contemporary works with a distinctive American voice. In 1990, HGO formed Opera New World, an ongoing program to produce new works that appeal to audiences that may have felt culturally, socially, or economically removed from the traditional opera. To date, HGO has produced 27 works under the auspices of Opera New World.

"We like to commission American operas for American audiences," Gockley says. "Traditional opera has been Eurocentric. We want to reflect America as it is today—with all its varied cultures and economics. We want our opera to express the many voices in America."

Tours and broadcasts have brought HGO productions international attention and acclaim, especially in 1996 when HGO's esteemed production of *Porgy and Bess* drew rave reviews at Opéra Bastille in France and La Scala in Italy, marking the company's debut at these famed opera houses.

Reaching the World through Multimedia

Gockley has worked hard to bring opera to a wider audience. HGO productions have been broadcast nationwide on PBS and are heard on National Public Radio's *World of Opera,* which is broadcast annually on 135 public radio stations nationwide.

In 1995, HGO debuted its Plazacast, which projects a live opera performance onto a giant outdoor screen outside the theater in Ray C. Fish Plaza. The Plazacast drew a diverse audience of 3,500 people to its debut performance of *La Cenerentola* and has become an annual event.

Gockley and HGO unveiled the Multimedia Modular Stage (MMS) in 1998 with a production of *Carmen* at The Cynthia Woods Mitchell Pavilion in the Woodlands and at the Miller Outdoor Theatre in Houston. The first of its kind for opera production, MMS is an attempt to take opera to the center of the community. The modular stage system, similar to stages used by traveling rock bands, utilizes three huge projection screens that receive still or moving prerecorded images,

MICHAEL HART

BRUCE BENNETT

The Wortham Theater Center (top), a $72 million state-of-the-art facility housing two theaters, has been the home of Houston Grand Opera since October 1987. In 1995, the company became the first in the United States to project a live performance—*La Cenerentola*, starring opera superstar Cecilia Bartoli—onto a giant outdoor screen for an audience of some 3,500 to enjoy free of charge.

JIM CALDWELL

and two huge video screens that receive live, up-close images of the performers.

The MMS *Carmen* performances reached more than 31,000 people of all ages, income levels, and cultural backgrounds, and the opera continues to hold these free performances. "At Miller Outdoor Theater in 1999, we reached more than 55,000 people with our performances. That's almost as many people as are attracted to their Fourth of July performance, which is Miller Theater's largest performance of the year," Gockley says. In June 2000, HGO's MMS production of *Pagliacci* traveled to The Cynthia Woods Mitchell Pavilion and the Mann Center in Philadelphia in addition to performances at Miller Theater.

KEN HOWARD

Inspiring Passion for Opera

The MMS is part of HGO's educational and community outreach initiatives, which are a progressive set of initiatives aimed at moving HGO closer to the center of community life. Also included in the initiatives are the Discovery Series; High School Night at the Opera, and Saturday Family Matinee, which offer operas at discounted rates for adults and students;

the Resident Artists Program, which brings artists into the community; STARS, a cross-curriculum and cross-cultural, award-winning arts program for students; and *Opera to Go!*, a local professional touring company, which presents fully-staged portable operas. The various education and outreach programs reach more than 150,000 people throughout the community annually.

In addition, HGO has established the

Houston Grand Opera Studio (HGOS), founded in 1977. HGOS is an established training program for young artists throughout the nation who have potential for careers in the opera/music theater profession.

"We want to infuse the community with the excitement and passion that opera offers us. Through our innovative programs and performances, we want people to see that, indeed, opera is for everyone," Gockley says.

Following in the footsteps of Houston Grand Opera's landmark 1976 production of *Porgy and Bess*, which captured Tony and Grammy awards, the 1995 production (top left) toured the United States, Japan, Italy, and France. One of the most popular of the opera's 25 world premieres, Daniel Catán's *Florencia en el Amazonas* (left) debuted in the 1996-1997 season. The organization operates under the leadership of music director Patrick Summers and general director David Gockley (top right, from left).

GEORGE HIXSON

With the June 1998 production of *Carmen*, the opera unveiled its state-of-the-art Multimedia Modular Stage, designed to bring live opera to mass audiences in outdoor venues, with an immediacy and impact equal to that of the theater.

© JIM OLIVE / STOCKYARD PHOTOS

CITY IN MOTION

1960-1972

1960

Houston Federal Credit Union

1962

Wheeler Avenue Baptist Church

1963

Unity National Bank

1967

Celanese Chemicals Clear Lake Plant

1967

St. Agnes Baptist Church

1968

Turner Construction

1970

City of Nassau Bay

1970

Lorance & Thompson, P.C.

1971

Houston Business Journal

1971

Houston Community College System

1972

Fort Bend Chamber of Commerce

Houston Federal Credit Union

It all started in 1960 as a way for Fluor Corporation's mid-continent employees to save money and secure loans. Originally chartered as Fluor Mid-Continent Employees Federal Credit Union, the name changed in 1966 to Fluor Houston Employees Federal Credit Union to include all employees of the Fluor Corporation.

Digicon Federal Credit Union merged with the credit union in 1986, and the name was changed to Houston Federal Credit Union. In 1988, Compaq Computer Corporation joined the credit union's field of membership. Throughout the years, companies continued to join the credit union as a way of offering affordable, convenient, and reliable financial services to their employees and families. The name Houston Federal Credit Union (HFCU) remains today and represents the strong, diverse field of membership the credit union serves.

Strength, Stability, Service

HFCU has grown from a small organization into a full-service financial institution, while still maintaining the level of quality service that members have come to expect. By the end of 1999, the credit union had served nearly 35,000 members with more than 70 sponsoring companies and more than $140 million in assets. HFCU's diverse list of sponsor companies includes energy and engineering corporations, computer and technology companies, physician groups, construction companies, law firms, and a host of other specialized companies. Today, HFCU is ranked as one of the largest credit unions in the Houston area.

The credit union's home office is located in Sugar Land on the Lake Pointe Plaza campus in southwest Houston. Also serving the Houston area are offices at the Compaq campuses in north Houston and Cypress, and on Kirby Drive, convenient to the Texas Medical Center and Greenway Plaza. In addition, HFCU has an office located in Fluor's Greenville, South Carolina, facility. As a member of the Texas and National Shared Service Center Network, HFCU offers its members access to five Texas Credit Union Service Centers and more than 300 service center outlets across the country. These additional facilities give members convenient access to the credit union's services all across the country.

A major focus of providing services to members today is instant access to their accounts. "We offer some of the most innovative services available, including Internet banking, Visa CheckCards, and a variety of other services, enabling members to access their accounts 24 hours a day, seven days a week," says HFCU President Sally McKnight.

Today, HFCU's services are accessible and convenient to people in every part of the world. Through Houston Federal Credit Union's Web site at www.houstonfcu.org, members can easily stay in touch with the credit union, whether they live in Sugar Land or Saudi Arabia. Internet banking gives members the ability and convenience to access their accounts any time of the day or night from anywhere they live. The Web site also enables members to apply for loans on-line, research vehicle pricing, trade stocks, and use HFCU's financial tools and on-line calculators to manage all aspects of their personal finances, including figuring out how much money they will need for retirement.

Experiencing the Credit Union Difference

From the credit union's founders to the present leadership, HFCU has spent 40 years building and growing, improving and enhancing, developing and progressing, always with one goal—to meet members' needs for quality financial service.

While membership has increased and numerous financial products and services have been added through the years, HFCU has continued to be guided by its founding

Houston Federal Credit Union (HFCU) proudly supports the Child Identification Program raffle. Pictured here are (from left) President Sally McKnight, credit union member and raffle winner Don Russell, Vice President of Member Services Shelly Halvorsen, and Vice President of Funds Management & Compliance Ginny Grant (top).

HFCU's main office is located in Sugar Land on the Lake Pointe Plaza campus (bottom).

The HFCU branch located on Compaq Computer Corporation's main campus in north Houston offers drive-through convenience and ATM service.

principle of People Helping People. Employees and families of HFCU-sponsoring companies make the difference, and the organization credits its members for the institution's success. Members own the credit union, elect its leadership, and have a voice in the way the it is run. The board of directors and other committee members are volunteers and do not receive compensation for their leadership. "One of the unique differences that sets credit unions apart from other financial institutions is that credit unions are not-for-profit. All profits are returned to members in the form of lower interest rates on loans and other low-cost, or even no-cost, services," McKnight says. "Houston Federal Credit Union strives to offer members the services they need to make their lives easier. Our full line of affordable products and services is designed to help members achieve their financial goals."

Also part of the credit union difference is the personalized service offered by HFCU employees. Several members of the management team have been with the organization for as many as 20 years. "We enjoy what we do. We know the members, and we make a point to understand their circumstances and work with them to provide the best solutions to fit their individual needs. We go the extra step in serving our members," says Shelly Halvorsen, vice president of member service.

Employees go the extra step in helping the community as well. HFCU participates

HFCU representatives understand the importance of quality service, and go the extra mile to ensure members receive personal attention, valuable information, and professional assistance .

in activities throughout the year to raise money for the Children's Miracle Network, which benefits Memorial Hermann Hospital. Employees also support the United Way through voluntary contributions. For the past several years, HFCU has adopted a United Way family during the holiday season and participates in a yearly food drive. HFCU plays an active role in the Child Identification Program in conjunction with the Texas Credit Union League and the American Football Coaches Association. The

three-year program is designed to raise money through raffle sales to provide identification kits to millions of Texas schoolchildren.

The principles of self-help, cooperation, and democracy still rank high in the traditions and practices of HFCU. As the credit union celebrates its 41st anniversary in 2001, Houston Federal Credit Union will continue to provide opportunities and enhance the financial position of its member-owners in the cooperative spirit that is the foundation of the credit union movement.

Wheeler Avenue Baptist Church

Wheeler Avenue Baptist Church has its roots at Texas Southern University, where, in 1962, Reverend William A. Lawson served as director of the Baptist Student Union and as professor in the Chair of Bible. "In those days, students didn't have transportation, so a nearby church was needed," Lawson says. ● After failing to solicit interest from established churches, Lawson and 13 interested members started meeting in the home of Lawson and his wife, Audrey. From there, the church quickly blossomed in membership. Eventually, a small, white-framed church was purchased on Wheeler Avenue, situated in Houston's Third Ward. Under the leadership of Lawson, the church's congregation has grown to more than 5,000 parishioners who worship in a new sanctuary.

Clockwise from top:
Wheeler Avenue Baptist Church is led by Reverend William A. Lawson.

The parishioners of Wheeler Avenue Baptist Church are involved in a variety of community outreach projects, including the cleanup of Olivewood Cemetery.

"The church is responsible for nurturing the entire family. We seek to build the characters of the young so they can live productively as servants of God," Lawson says.

Rooted in Change

Wheeler Avenue Baptist Church—founded amidst the heat of the civil rights movement—was once deemed radical for its participation in sit-ins and demonstrations. Inspired by the teachings of Martin Luther King Jr., the church became the Houston chapter for the Southern Christian Leadership Conference.

Because they were once part of a downtown Houston theater that barred black citizens from entering, the doors of Wheeler Avenue Baptist Church carry significant symbolic importance for the congregation and the community. When segregation was outlawed, the theater owners made the choice to board over its doors and close down the theater, rather than allow blacks to enter the establishment.

Walking through those now-welcoming doors, families uphold and celebrate the church's commitment to challenging socio-economic deprivation, racism, illiteracy, injustice, and other social ills. The lack of adornment in the sanctuary is striking. No pillars or decorations distract from its atmosphere; no stained glass windows distort the color of the outside light. After Lawson's sermon, the awnings that cover the clear glass windows are opened, and the sanctuary is bathed in natural light.

Stewards of God

Outside the sanctuary are the housing projects, the suffering, and the injustice of the world. "I want the congregation to respond to the outside world—to take responsibility for their fellow man the way God has taken responsibility for them," Lawson says. "We've always been advocates for the poor and disenfranchised.

"We have a responsibility to our congregation, to the neighborhood in which we reside, and to the community," Lawson continues. "It's the responsibility of the strong to help shoulder the burdens of the weak. We are all human beings with flaws and imperfections, but we seek to help human beings reach their highest potential as servants of God."

Wheeler's outreach activities are numerous and far-reaching. Its character-building ministries include youth-related outreach such as Boy Scouts, Girl Scouts, Young Life, rites-of-passage ministry, a tutoring program, and an infants' school. "The church is responsible for nurturing the entire family. We seek to build the characters of the young so they can live productively as servants of God," Lawson says.

For the indigent, Wheeler has an emergency outreach program similar to the United Way and the American Red Cross. "Through our missions and mercy ministry, we raise about $250,000 each year from our congregation. That money goes toward providing emergency funds for people in need. We'll help them pay rent, get their lights back on, and provide food and clothing. The program is geared toward helping people get back on their feet," Lawson says.

The church's long-time Meals on Wheels ministry works in conjunction with neighborhood centers to provide more than 300 meals each day to senior citizens. "We have several stations in neighborhoods and are served mostly by volunteers that get out there each and every day. That dedication to service is what our congregation is all about," Lawson says.

Rehabilitating the lives of people in the community is another extension of the church's outreach. The church has been active in its jail and prison ministry and its substance abuse ministry for many years, and is now seeking to form a ministry for juveniles in trouble. On an international level, the church has established ministries in Haiti and in Africa.

Wheeler's HIV/AIDS care team provides social, emotional, and spiritual support to people with HIV/AIDS, while the church's cancer ministry counsels cancer survivors and/or family members affected both directly and indirectly by the disease.

In addition to its partnership in establishing a neighborhood shopping center and additional jobs, Wheeler was also involved in establishing Inner City Visions, a nonprofit organization that seeks to provide affordable housing in the neighborhood. "We need to be a positive force for providing affordable and safe housing for the citizens in our community," Lawson says. "We can't forget the world outside our windows.

"With God at the center of all we do, we can be stewards of him, making a positive impact in the church, in our neighborhoods, and in the communities in which we live."

Wheeler Avenue Baptist Church has grown from a small, white-framed church with 13 members to a congregation of more than 5,000 parishioners who worship in a new sanctuary (top right).

For its anniversary celebration, the church holds services at Texas Southern University (top left).

The church also hosts a wide variety of activities for its congregation, including a banquet on Valentine's Day (middle).

Wheeler Avenue Baptist Church was instrumental in coordinating a peaceful march to protest state funding inequalities between the University of Texas and two historically black universities, Texas Southern University and Prairie View A&M University (bottom).

Since opening in 1963 as a small community bank dedicated to serving underserved residents of Houston, Unity National Bank hasn't wavered from its mission of tailoring its services to the community. Through hard work and a clear set of priorities, Unity is entering the new millennium with a growing customer base and a solid balance sheet, allowing the bank to offer a complete range of products and services at competitive rates. ● Headquartered on Blodgett in the heart of Houston's historical Third Ward, Unity is the only bank in Texas owned and managed by African-Americans. Founded as Riverside National Bank, the institution became Unity National Bank in 1985 after being purchased by Bayshore Bank Corp.

Its current owners, a group of churches and individuals, purchased the bank in 1989. Since then, Unity has remained under solid management, expanding its product line and services to remain competitive, while continuing to gear its loans toward programs and businesses that benefit the community. Unity specializes in small busi-

Susan Borches is vice president of corporate affairs for Shell Community Initiative. The Shell Community Banking Initiative, a subsidiary of Shell Oil Company, is partnering with Unity National Bank to pilot an innovative community banking project that will help the bank to further extend its lending capabilities to small businesses (top).

Unity's main branch is located in the historic Third Ward (bottom).

ness loans that aid in community redevelopment, mortgage loans, and home improvement loans, as well as auto loans. "Our business lending philosophy encourages the use of various agencies to increase and enhance the possibilities of loan approval," says Larry Hawkins, president and CEO. Because of the bank's commitment, the U.S. Small Business Administration designated Unity as a certified lender. The bank was also recognized by the Independent Bankers Association of Texas as one of the outstanding community banks in the state.

Community Investments

In addition to making loans that help businesses establish themselves in the area, Unity has been a trailblazer in implementing the Community Reinvestment Act (CRA), which requires banks to make loans in communities where they take deposits. Unity works closely with agencies and organizations—such as the YMCA, NAACP, Boy Scouts of America, and Third Ward Development Council— to build or redevelop facilities in order to launch community programs, hold meetings, or sponsor courses.

"We follow the spirit of CRA above and beyond what the law calls for," says Tommy Brooks, executive vice president and CFO. "We have been designated a Community Development Bank by the Office of the Comptroller of the Currency (OCC), and as a Community Development Financial Institution by the United States Department of the Treasury, which means that our primary focus is to serve community needs." In keeping with the spirit of the CRA, Unity has created products specifically designed for residents on fixed or limited incomes. Senior citizens or college students can open checking accounts with low minimum deposits and nominal service fees. To help support area schools, Unity offers customers the Education Reinvestment account, in which a portion of the service fees are donated to customers' selected schools in the Houston and Fort Bend independent school districts.

In addition to its lending program and specialized products, Unity is an active force of change in the community. Bank employees are visible community volunteers, participating in neighborhood cleanups and food drives, tutoring and career day programs at nearby schools, and supporting United Way and Junior Achievement activities.

Unity's Fort Bend branch opened in 1998.

Business Partnerships

Alliances with community organizations and corporations are key to the bank's long-term success. In the 1990s, Unity formed strong business partnerships with HEB Pantry Foods, the National Bankers' Association, and Bank of America. Also, Salomon Smith Barney, a financial services corporation, has a financial consultant on-site at Unity. Wells Fargo Bank has made an investment in Unity to enhance the bank's ability to make community redevelopment loans.

The Shell Community Banking Initiative, a subsidiary of Shell Oil Company, is partnering with Unity to pilot an innovative community banking project that will help the bank to further extend its lending capabilities to small businesses. "Partnerships such as these help to validate who we are and keep Unity strong," says Hawkins. Customers like Harlon Brooks (Harlon's BBQ) and Brian Smith (Brian Smith Construction) have also

helped Unity to stay strong by committing major projects and resources to the bank.

Superior Customer Service

In addition to traditional financial products and services, Unity offers automated teller machines, Visa check cards, and other progressive products. But what helps the small, privately owned financial institution hold its stake in today's era of mega-banks is its superior customer service philosophy. From the pot of coffee brewing in the bank lobby to the friendly welcome from the lobby receptionist, Unity's atmosphere emits a feeling of warmth and community. Bank employees know their customers—most of whom have banked at the facility for decades—by name.

"We see our customers as individuals, not as numbers," says Deborah Archie, senior vice president and cashier. "When customers come to Unity, we sit down with them and discuss their circumstances in order to find

ways to meet their needs. Our philosophy is to make sound, sensible banking decisions with the individual in mind."

Millennium Goals

As Unity National Bank enters the 21st century, it continues to grow and increase its services to meet customer demand. In 1998, Unity opened a second branch southwest of Houston, on Texas Parkway in Missouri City. With 11 officers and 26 employees, Unity's goal is to continue its expansion with the opening of multiple branches throughout Houston, as well as the launching of an Internet Web site.

Unity National Bank remains committed to its original mission. "We intend to continue doing what we do best, which is to provide convenient and professional services to all our customers," says Hawkins. "Our vision is to become the Bank of Choice throughout underserved communities where we have a physical presence."

Customers such as Brian Smith (Brian Smith Construction) and Harlon Brooks (Harlon's BBQ) have helped Unity stay strong in the community by committing major projects and resources to the bank.

Celanese Chemicals Clear Lake Plant

For almost a century, Celanese has been quietly manufacturing the basic building blocks for a variety of everyday products, from paints, adhesives, detergents, and cosmetics to fibers, plastics, and textile products. With more than 30 facilities worldwide, the company is a global leader in the production of commodity chemicals, acetate products, and engineering plastics. Operating in the Houston area since 1967, the Celanese Chemicals Clear Lake Plant is dedicated to quality, safety, health, and environmental issues, making it a responsible neighbor in the community. The plant is located on more than 1,000 acres of land in an industrial district of Pasadena, and employs approximately 900 people, including full-time and contract workers. It is a world leader in the production of bulk commodity chemicals, and provides products to other petrochemical companies, specialty chemical companies, and consumer products companies around the globe.

A continuous program of innovation and improvement has increased the plant's capacity to more than 5 billion pounds annually. The Clear Lake Plant is specifically engineered for synergistic production—chemicals and by-products of one production unit are used in the production of other chemicals. This synergy increases efficiency, minimizes waste, and helps ensure quality. The plant has world-scale facilities, and has a long roster of customers and business partners in Houston and around the globe. Products are shipped to customers via pipeline, oceangoing tankers, barges, rail, and highway tank trucks.

Proactive Environmental Measures

The Clear Lake plant is a leader in environmental, health, and safety performance. Its proactive environmental and safety programs have received recognition from state organizations, including the Texas Natural Resource Conservation Commission (TNRCC), and by industry organizations, such as the Chemical Manufacturers Association (CMA), the Texas Chemical Council (TCC), and the National Petroleum Refiners Association (NPRA).

"We work in full cooperation with regulatory agencies," says Site Director Jim S. Alder. "We consider them valued partners in our joint effort to produce essential materials in a safe and responsible manner. We strive to identify problems and initiate action before concerns arise."

Celanese Clear Lake is proud of its record of waste minimization and its sensitivity to environmental concerns. The plant has achieved an 85 percent reduction in Toxic Release Inventory (TRI) emissions over the past five years.

A Leader in Safety

The Clear Lake site's safety record has consistently ranked among the industry's best. It conducts regular

Celanese Chemicals Clear Lake Plant is located in a Pasadena industrial district in southeast Houston.

Deer are among the many wildlife inhabitants that roam the Celanese Chemicals Clear Lake Plant property.

safety drills and education programs, and abides by strict enforcement of safety rules. Through strong management emphasis and employee involvement, the plant has reduced serious injuries by more than 80 percent over the past decade. During the same time period, it has reduced the plant OSHA incident rate from near eight to less than 1.5.

"Our employees have made this happen," Alder says. "Their dedication to safety is paramount to the success of the Clear Lake plant."

Dedication to Community Awareness

The plant's unique location gives it a neighborly responsibility to four communities: the Clear Lake area, Pasadena, Deer Park, and La Porte. Therefore, it strives to keep citizens in these communities aware of its activities and to address local concerns.

As a participant in CMA's Responsible Care program, the plant takes part in community advisory panels, which provide a forum for citizens to talk with their industrial neighbors. "As a good neighbor, our doors are open to the community. Citizens have a right to know what we do and how we do it," Alder says. "We regularly answer questions citizens have and provide information or tours as requested."

The Celanese plant is also a member of several chambers of commerce, manufacturing associations, and community service organizations. It actively participates in organizations such as Channel Industry Mutual Aid (CIMA), East Harris County Manufacturers Association (EHCMA), and the Community Awareness Emergency Response (CAER) initiative.

The plant's charitable activities focus on sponsorship and participation in organizations such as United Way, American Heart Association, Boys and Girls Harbor, American Red Cross, Susan G. Komen Breast Cancer Foundation, and Juvenile Diabetes Foundation.

Plant workers also share the company's commitment to reach out to the community. In 1999, the plant invested more than $300,000 and 2,000 employee volunteer hours in organizations located in its surrounding communities. Educational outreach activities include mentoring, scholarship programs, Junior Achievement instruction, and the Texas Scholars program. Additionally, every year, the plant's employees participate in several environmental cleanup events, including the Armand Bayou Nature Center Trash Bash and the University of Houston Household Hazardous Waste Day.

"We're proud not only to be leaders in our industry, but also to be proactive in environmental, health, safety, and community concerns," Alder says. "It's all part of being a good and responsible neighbor."

Clockwise from top:
Celanese Chemicals Clear Lake Plant employees and family members gather at the University of Houston-Clear Lake to participate in the Juvenile Diabetes Foundation Walk to Cure Diabetes fund-raiser.

Process operator Lori Everett discusses piping layout with operators Darryl Carpenter and Melba Rodriguez on the new Acrylic Acid II distillation towers at the Clear Lake plant.

Senior Process Control Engineer Deborah Jackson reviews control interface graphics for the new Acrylic Acid II unit at the Clear Lake plant.

When the Reverend Gene A. Moore Sr. and Houston missionary Mary Agnes Foster were alerted to the need for a church in the burgeoning South Acres Estates community in 1967, they took to the streets, asking residents to join in their quest. What came out of those walks was a fellowship of six members who met in a home. Today, more than 33 years later, the seeds of that fellowship have grown into a worship community of more than 12,000 members. St. Agnes Baptist Church, named after Foster, has emerged as a significant spiritual presence in the Houston community. ● Through its spiritual teachings, ministry programs, and educational and community outreach, the church seeks to empower its members to live the Gospel in every sector of their lives. "The March of Faith Ministries of St. Agnes Baptist Church is an evangelistic tool with a mission to help develop the 'total man' with the gospel of Jesus Christ. The word of God is used to bond men, women, and children from all cultures, races, and nationalities. The word affirms the truth and bears witness to the supreme power of God, which can restore and revive all of us for victorious living," Moore says.

The Vision of Dome City

The March of Faith Ministries is reaching a culmination in Moore's vision of Dome City, an ambitious multi-dome spiritual facility set on the church's 137-acre campus. "We want to equip individuals for Christlike leadership in the home, community, nation, and world," Moore says. "Dome City will offer hope and restoration for the lives of many people and prepare them for effective living in their homes and community."

The church plans to construct several domes, using monolithic dome architecture. With this style of architecture, dome-shaped tents are inflated and reinforced

▼ FERRELL PHELPS

with concrete to create a self-supporting structure that not only carries tremendous acoustics, but is also resistant to hurricane, floods, and tornadoes.

The March of Faith Dome Cathedral, set for completion in December 2000, will be the nucleus of Dome City. More than 200 feet wide and 50 feet tall, the cathedral will act as the main worship center. Another dome, the Dome of Restoration, will be a multipurpose center aimed primarily at "mending the broken man and restoring him to a life of productivity and fruitfulness," according to Moore. By offering an alternative way of living—free from substance abuse, joblessness, and other emotional bondage—this center will combine evangelism and counseling with educational techniques and behavioral skills for retooling, restructuring, and redirecting people's lives.

The Domes of Refuge will seek to shelter those in need, providing temporary housing and a transitional system for senior citizens, single mothers, and economically disadvantaged adults. The Dome of Recreation and Family Life Center will be a multipurpose facility for 24-hour entertainment and physical recreation.

And the Dome of Renewal/Education will offer a broad scope of educational and tutorial programs, as well as instructional

Reverend Gene A. Moore Sr. is co-founder of St. Agnes Baptist Church.

▼ FERRELL PHELPS

St. Agnes Baptist Church promotes fellowship in the community it serves.

and technical skills for shaping both youth and adults. Structured within this unique educational program will be a seminary for ministerial training and a continuing education center. In addition, Dome City will house several area small businesses and a medical clinic.

Serving the Houston Community

The church remains active in its educational, community, and economic outreach. Since 1981, the church has been working to foster the educational well-being of the community through St. Agnes Christian Academy. The school now offers classes in grades K-7 and is progressing towards a complete high school facility.

The Foundation for Economic and Educational Development and the Small Business Incubator Initiative seek to provide small-business owners with facilities and training for economic growth. The Gregoreo School, an affiliate of Friends International Christian University, is a unique college on the campus of St. Agnes Baptist Church. The school offers undergraduate and graduate degrees for ministry and other fields of study. In addition, the church works in conjunction with organizations such as the Houston Food Bank to provide food, clothes, and shelter to people in need.

Since 1988, St. Agnes has been broadcasting its services on television. With production facilities located on site, the program reaches more than 25 million homes.

In its continual spiritual outreach, the church has created a satellite worship center in Pearland and is looking to build satellite churches in other Texas communities, such as Lake Jackson and League City. "We at St. Agnes Baptist Church are pioneers, unafraid to take a leap of faith. Dome City is a beacon to a confused world. We are seeking to bring the Kingdom of God to earth, creating an atmosphere for total spiritual development and healing," Moore says.

▲ TONY GAINES

Through its spiritual teachings, ministry programs, and educational and community outreach, the church seeks to empower its members to live the Gospel in every sector of their lives.

▲ TONY GAINES

Moore and Reverend Jesse Jackson discuss current issues at a political summit on the church campus.

Turner Construction

From the steps of New York's first subway line in 1903, to overseas American air bases during World War II, to Madison Square Garden in 1965, to the Republic Bank Center (now NationsBank) in Houston in 1982, Turner Construction has been building America. And now, in the dawn of a new century, the local company is poised to build the infrastructure for a new tomorrow. With a presence in Houston since 1968, Turner's cornerstone for success lies in the words of Turner himself: "We are awarded most of our work based on reputation. Preservation of our reputation demands a commitment to quality, service, and

operating within approved budgets and schedules. This commitment is the foundation of our company." With 60 percent of its business coming from repeat clients, it's clear Turner's words ring true even today.

Always Committed to Quality

Convinced that steel-bar reinforced concrete—called the Ransome system—was a faster, less expensive way to build than the wood-frame and masonry methods used at the time, Henry C. Turner and DeForrest H. Dixon founded Turner Construction Company in 1902, helping to

usher in a new era in construction. They founded the company on three core values—service, quality, and integrity. These values have guided the company through the years, and this commitment has helped make Turner the largest commercial general contractor in the United States. With executive management based in Dallas, the company has a network of offices in 41 cities throughout the United States. A recent merger with HOCHTIEF, Germany's largest construction company with a worldwide presence, secures Turner as a leader not only in the United States, but also around the globe.

The company's project experience is vast. "You'd be hard pressed to find a building type we haven't yet constructed," says Vice President and General Manager Kyle Rooney. Turner is the nation's leading health care builder and has been one of *Fortune* magazine's Most Admired Companies in its industry ranking, based on solid earnings, record sales, and strong employee performance.

Locally, the company is responsible for the two tallest buildings in Houston, the Texas Commerce Bank (now Chase Bank) Tower, and the Allied Bank Plaza, as well as the city's largest building complex, the Allen Center. "We pride ourselves on offering our clients a unique combination of

national expertise in both preconstruction and construction phase services, coupled with a strong local presence," Rooney says.

With more than 30 years' experience in Texas, Turner's powerhouse list of clients includes Texas A&M University, University of Texas, Hines Interests, Century Development, Exxon Mobil, U.S. Sprint, and General Electric. Its Houston and Dallas offices complete approximately $200 million in work annually. The company's services include general contracting, construction management, preconstruction, construction monitoring, design-build, design-build/finance, program management, construction consulting, and national building programs.

In addition to major corporations and small industrial and commercial clients, Turner

Some of Turner Construction's most notable projects in the Houston area include (from top) Bank of America Tower, Allied Bank Plaza, and Shell Woodcreek Office Complex.

serves a wide array of public and private institutions. Its construction versatility is reflected in some of its recent projects, which include manufacturing facilities, campus projects, tenant finishes, office buildings, hospitals, retail centers, schools, civic centers, industrial plants, laboratories, and warehouses.

The company completes approximately 1,000 projects nationwide each year and takes pride in cataloging its accomplishments in *Turner City*, an annual publication that compiles a list of all construction projects completed during the year in a fictitious city.

According to Rooney, Turner's success in the Houston area stems from its home-grown talent. "We are Houston-operated, and our people know the business locally," Rooney says. The Houston office is staffed by approximately 100 employees, including project executives, project managers, engineers, superintendents, estimators, cost/scheduling engineers, accountants, and sales/marketing/contract specialists.

Local Presence, International Expertise

Turner's strength in the industry lies in its ability to deliver personalized service with a knowledge and understanding of how to complete a high-quality project on time and within budget. The company is a leader in cost analysis: Its quarterly *Turner Building Cost Index* is used nationwide as a pricing guide for construction services. "Even our competitors use it," Rooney says.

The company's emphasis on "getting it right the first time" is evident in its commitment to preconstruction services. "Once a project is in the field, a mistake can double or triple an original estimate. Our job is to make sure those mistakes are caught before they reach the field," Rooney says. "Guiding our clients through the pitfalls and minefields of a project is what we're here for. Our ability to complete projects on time and within

Turner has helped to shape the downtown Houston skyline with such buildings as Chase Bank Tower and Bank of America Tower.

Turner has constructed a wide variety of projects for Exxon.

budget is a hallmark of Turner." During the preconstruction planning phase, Turner staff provides advice on building systems, materials, and construction techniques, as well as detailed cash-flow analysis, scheduling options, and constructibility and logistics reviews.

The company remains dedicated to a personalized approach to construction, recognizing that understanding the client's needs is paramount to Turner's success. Rooney explains that while Turner is locally run, the company can draw from a broad pool of expertise around the globe. "If we haven't constructed a particular type of building," he says, "you can bet someone in our com-

pany has. The company's strength lies in its ability to pull in experts when needed, while maintaining local control over a project. That's what sets us apart from the competition. That's what we call the Turner Advantage."

Turner takes pride in being one of the leaders in sustainable construction, wherein recycled building-content materials are used whenever possible. "It's a new world, and we have to broaden our services to stay on top of our clients' changing needs," Rooney says. The company constructed one of the first buildings to use this method, the Rose Garden Arena in Oregon, home of the Portland Trailblazers.

Fostering Partnerships

According to Rooney, a general contractor is not only responsible for delivering top service to its clients, but must also foster successful partnerships with its subcontractors. "We are only as strong as our weakest link. Making sure we maintain these relationships is crucial to our project success," he says.

To ensure successful partnerships with subcontractors, the company abides strictly by four rules of conduct. The bidding process must be fair and equitable. The contract document must not favor the general contractor, but must be fair to both sides. The work in the field must be coordinated properly so individual subcontractors can perform their work without interruption. And the subcontractor must be paid promptly after the work has been completed to the satisfaction of the project team. "Having a local staff in place that understands the people in the area and is committed to these four rules of conduct is essential," Rooney says.

Strength in Diversity

Since the 1960s, Turner has been widely recognized on the local and national levels for its proactive support of minority- and women-owned business enterprises (M/WBE). The company is an active member of many local organizations that support this issue, including the Houston Minority Business Council and the Houston Minority Business Development Center, as well as local chapters of the Urban League, National Association of Minority Contractors, and Women Contractor's Association.

Turner's M/WBE Construction Management Training Program, a partnership with

Turner's technical expertise has been crucial in a variety of high-tech projects in Houston, including the construction of St. Joseph Hospital.

the City of Houston, has received significant recognition. This special construction management program for local M/WBEs centers on the primary construction functions of owning and operating a successful construction company. The program covers topics such as estimating and bidding, safety, contracts and purchasing, bonding and insurance, establishing and managing credit, project management, and marketing. Since its inception in 1992, more than 200 M/WBEs have successfully completed the program, and Turner has awarded contracts to more than 200 M/WBEs as well. In recognition of its efforts, the company has been recognized several times by the City of Houston with a special Turner Construction Day.

Nationally, Turner's commitment to the enhancement of minority and women business enterprises has earned the company an Exemplary Voluntary Effort award from the U.S. Department of Labor, a United States Congressional Salute, Corporation of the Year award from the U.S. Department of Commerce, and several Major Corporation of the Year awards from the National Association of Minority Contractors.

In addition to its M/WBE efforts, the company is very active in recruiting and cooperative programs. "We want to recruit employees who know Texas," Rooney says—so every company recruiter must be an alumnus of the university with which he or she works. The company has a strong recruiting presence at the University of Texas, Texas A&M University, Texas Tech, and Prairie View A&M, and employs several student interns in its co-op program.

For more than 30 years, the company has played a part not only in building the Houston area, but also in the success of many annual charity events. In addition to its sponsorship of the Houston Livestock Show and Rodeo, the company is active in the Muscular Dystrophy Bowlathon, the March of Dimes Walkathon, and the Soapbox Derby. "We're not just building better infrastructure for the Houston area. We're committed to building a better community as well," Rooney says.

Turner's projects also include the Texas A&M Foundation Headquarters in College Station and the 1010 Lamar building in Houston.

There was a time when the residents of the city of Nassau Bay were always looking to the stars. Incorporated in 1970, the city was originally built to support its internationally recognized neighbor, NASA's Johnson Space Center. Since that time, more than 60 astronauts—some of whom walked on the moon— have called Nassau Bay home. ● Today, the residents of Nassau Bay still look to the stars—but also keep an eye on the local scenery. It's hard to miss the growth potential of what has become a major recreational and business region. A newly formed economic development organization is repositioning Nassau Bay for the new millennium with a vision of rebirth. Focused on a plan to create a galleria-style international retail center that will be complemented by new and updated office complexes, the city is reaching for new heights.

The Clear Lake Region: A Recreational Mecca

Nestled in the Clear Lake region, a mere 25 miles south of downtown Houston, Nassau Bay is bordered by Space Center Houston, the official visitors' center of the Johnson Space Center. With attractions such as Space Center Theater and the Feel of Space, Space Center Houston is the second-largest-attended tourist facility in the state of Texas.

The city also borders Clear Lake, a 1,728-acre natural inlet that combines the waters of Clear Creek and Galveston Bay. With more than 23 marinas and 10,000 boating slips, Clear Lake boasts the largest concentration of pleasure boats in the United States and is the boating capital of the state.

A proposed convention center—which would house a hotel, a space education facility, a golf course, and other components— would draw even more visitors to the Clear Lake region.

Nassau Bay's vision of its retail sector includes the representation of the coun-tries involved in the space program. A sister city to Star City, Russia—home to Russia's equivalent of Johnson Space Center— for more than six years, Nassau Bay understands the importance of cultural diversity. Largely because of the development of the International Space Station, the Johnson Space Center has become a melting pot of different countries and cultures around the world. By establishing a retail center that is international, the city is sharing in the wealth of the nations that helped make the area and the space program what they are today.

The city plans to make way for upscale waterfront businesses, restaurants, and cultural arts centers, and is developing the infrastructure to support a wide array of retail industries. Nassau Bay has the residential support and the visitor population to make this development a success. It's a win-win scenario for the community.

Diversity in Business

Since the Johnson Space Center was established in the early 1960s, the Clear Lake region has become home to more than 7,000 businesses, including aerospace, biotech, software, and other high-tech companies. Nassau Bay has been

Space Center Houston is a major tourist attraction in Texas, drawing visitors from around the world (left).

Nassau Bay is the cultural arts center of the bay area, and home of Clear Creek County Theatre, the Arts Alliance, and the Clear Lake Symphony (right).

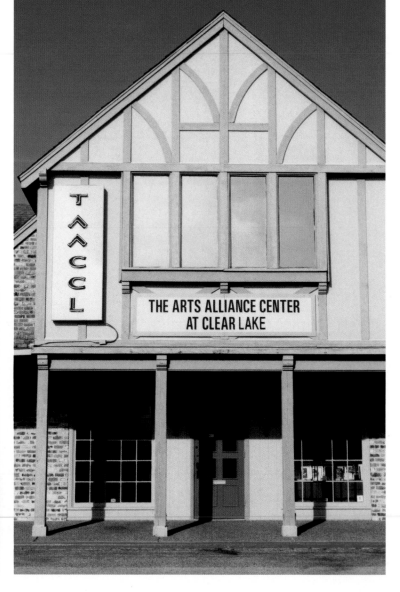

THE ARTS ALLIANCE CENTER AT CLEAR LAKE

revitalizing its office complexes and offers a wide array of office space for companies needing just a few support offices, as well as for businesses wanting build-to-suit options. The city can accommodate a variety of office needs, and with the newly formed economic development organization, is positioned to offer the incentives necessary to bring businesses to Nassau Bay.

As charter members, the city is closely aligned with the Clear Lake Area Economic Development Foundation and the Clear Lake Convention and Visitors Bureau. With 11 cities represented in the Clear Lake region, there is a tremendous cooperative spirit, and companies relocating to the region

can work, live, and play, all in one area.

With more than 1,400 residences and an average annual household income of more than $100,000, Nassau Bay provides an upscale residential community with many waterfront living accommodations. The neighborhood boasts one of the leading school districts in the state—Clear Creek Independent School District—and the abundance of high-tech companies in the region has attracted many well-educated, skilled professionals.

The city is also proud of its involvement in the arts and is considered the arts center of the Clear Lake region. Nassau Bay has held an arts festival in celebration of its Russian

sister city, and expects to expand its cultural reach with the development of an annual international arts festival, as well as other cultural and artistic activities. Nassau Bay is also home to the Clear Creek County Theater, and is an active supporter of the Clear Lake Arts Alliance Center, which is the umbrella organization for the Clear Lake Symphony, Clear Lake Metropolitan Ballet, Bay Area Symphony League, Clear Creek County Theatre, and others.

There is a tremendous level of growth on the horizon, and the City of Nassau Bay is committed to aggressively redeveloping the area into an important cultural, retail, and business sector for the Clear Lake region.

NASA

NASA

Nassau Bay's major employers are engaged in a full range of space operations, including flying the space shuttle and building the International Space Station.

Lorance & Thompson, P.C.

As one of the preeminent law firms in the Houston area, Lorance & Thompson, P.C. has built a reputation not only on its many courtroom victories, but also on the degree of personalized service rendered by its team of seasoned professionals. The firm has been in business since 1970 and continues to enjoy steady growth. With the addition of a new office in Laredo, the firm is positioning itself for the new millennium. ●

When its founders, Tom Lorance and Larry Thompson, first opened the firm's doors, they specialized in the broad field of tort and insurance litigation. Today, in response to growing and changing litigation needs, the firm has diversified its expertise.

Among its general practice services are transportation law, products liability and litigation, health and managed care law, civil appellate law, insurance litigation, and environmental/toxic tort litigation.

Lorance & Thompson's attorneys represent major businesses, government agencies, individuals, and insurers in a broad range of matters, from relatively simple personal injury matters to highly complex multiparty cases.

The firm's reach extends across Texas; its attorneys practice before all levels of state trial and appellate courts. Its federal practice handles cases in all four Texas districts, as well as appellate work in the U.S. Court of Appeals for the Fifth Circuit and in the U.S. Supreme Court.

A Network of Professionals

The representation of transportation companies and their insurance carriers has long been a significant part of Lorance & Thompson's practice. The new Laredo office will focus primarily on transportation law, mostly representing trucking companies. "More trucks cross the border in Laredo than any other place in the nation." says Trey Williams, head of the firm's transportation sector. "We saw a need for skilled transportation lawyers in that area, and we are prepared to meet it."

The firm's attorneys are active in local, state, and national transportation industry trade groups. This participation is in recognition of the ever growing need for defense counsel who are both knowledgeable of and sensitive to the business side of the transportation industry.

Furthermore, a network of additional legal expertise is at the firm's fingertips. As a founding member of the American Law Firm Association (ALFA), Lorance & Thompson is able to call on the experience of more than 100 firms throughout the United States, as well as a dozen countries. "The network is an invaluable resource. In areas where we may not have a specialist, we can gain the legal advice from a wide array of experts," says Thompson, president of the firm. Through ALFA's E-mail system, the firm can get answers typically within a single day.

Well-Utilized Resources

Lorance & Thompson has integrated state-of-the-art technology into its courtroom presentations. The firm regularly makes use of computer graphics, video, and multimedia technology. "The days of flowery oratory are gone," Thompson explains. "Winning a trial involves presenting

Lorance & Thompson, P.C.'s (from left) Michael Blaise, David Prasifka, and Trey Williams study the numbers.

◄ KEL THOMPSON

▲ KEL THOMPSON

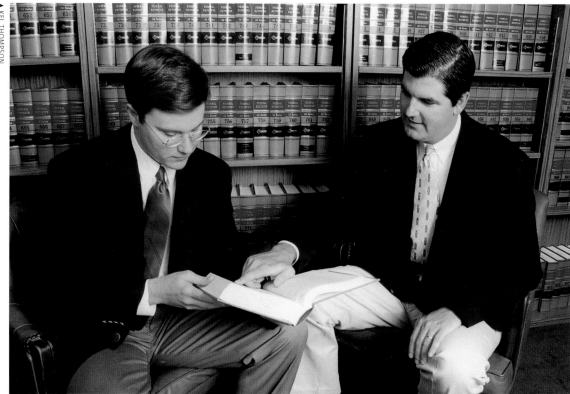

Todd Trombley (left) and Wayne Little
go to the books to check a fact.

the facts in the most clear and concise way."

The firm's dedication to clients is another reason it has gained such a solid reputation in the Houston area. "We are available 24 hours a day, seven days a week," Thompson says. "Many problems just cannot wait until regular office hours. Going above and beyond the call of duty is a way of life for us."

For example, the firm has established a health care department with a rotating call system for its hospital clients. "If a hospital risk manager has a patient crisis on a Saturday night, access to legal counsel is never more than a call away," he says.

The firm's attorneys also offer continuing education seminars for clients such as doctors, nurses, claims adjusters, and risk managers. "Many professionals need a

very active and working knowledge of the law," Thompson says. "Through regularly scheduled seminars, we can keep these clients on top of legal changes in their respective fields, providing an invaluable resource to others within the community."

Numerous Accolades

The firm's successes have earned Lorance & Thompson numerous accolades. It has consistently received an AV rating by Martindale-Hubbell, the nation's primary rating service of law firms and lawyers. The rating is the top ranking given to law firms in the United States.

"All lawyers are listed in the Martindale-Hubbell directory, but not all law firms are rated," Thompson says. "The AV rating

reflects the firm's excellence and expertise in the practice of law."

The majority of the firm's 16 lawyers are board certified in civil trial law or personal injury law, and several are certified in both fields. They stay active in professional organizations, engaging in speeches and writing articles for trade journals. In addition, they participate in numerous community organizations.

"It's essential for our lawyers not only to stay on top of changes in the industry, but also to remain in touch with the needs of the community," Thompson says. "Lorance & Thompson has succeeded in the Houston area for so long because we are dedicated not only to serving our clients, but also to serving the City of Houston as a whole."

▲ KEL THOMPSON

Attorneys (from left) Prasifka, Blaise,
Diane Guariglia, and William Luyties
prepare for an upcoming case.

To be successful in business, one must stay informed about what's happening in the local economy, the marketplace, and the competition. For more than 20 years, Houston entrepreneurs, business owners, and corporate executives in an array of industries have read the *Houston Business Journal* to get that information.

"On average, our readers spend about half an hour each week reading our paper," Publisher John Beddow says. "That's half an hour out of their business life. Businesspeople spend their time trying to develop new business, finding competitive advantages, or learning about their clients. So the fact that we have a product people are willing to spend a significant amount of time with says a lot about the insight we offer into the Houston business world."

Building a Connection

Founded in 1971 by television broadcaster Bob Gray, the *Houston Business Journal* was bought by American City Business Journals in 1986. In addition to more than 41 journals across the country, American City runs Street & Smith Sports Group, which publishes three motorsports periodicals, *SportsBusiness Journal*, and five sports annuals. It is a division of Advance Publications, Inc., which also operates Condé Nast Magazines, *The New Yorker*, Newhouse Newspapers, and several cable television operations.

Reporting on local and business-to-business news, as well as feature articles, Editor Bill Schadewald leads a staff of reporters at the *Houston Business Journal* who seek out, examine, and present factual news that affects all types of area businesses.

"Bill is highly regarded in the local business community as someone who has seen the city through many periods, from the bust in the early 1980s to the difficult times that followed as the city pulled itself up by its bootstraps and diversified," Beddow says.

Today, Schadewald's expert team covers a wide variety of beats, including real estate, technology, health care, retail, securities, marketing, and media, as well as a new beat called business and government, which examines the effects of decisions made by area governments on the local business scene. American City Business Journals also has a Washington bureau that supplies information to each local journal, keeping readers up to date on Capitol Hill news.

Along with the local and national business news, the *Houston Business Journal's* For the Record section lists bankruptcies, offers information on upcoming seminars, and provides information on loans and banking. Each issue features a profile of a key Houston businessperson—anyone from an operator of a tie-dyed T-shirt shop to an owner of a $10 million software venture.

"The current editorial staff is the most seasoned I've had in my career. They each average about five or six years of experience," Schadewald says. "The main thing that separates us from the city's daily newspaper is that we are proactive rather than reactive in our approach to covering business news."

Giving readers another way to access up-to-the-minute information, the *Houston Business Journal's* Web site, www.bizjournals.com/houston, features the latest in business news, in addition to a wide variety of services aimed at supplementing readers' subscriptions. Future plans for the site include a customization feature that will allow readers to view only the news they need, stock tickers, Webcasts of important events, and polls and surveys on local business issues.

Appealing to the "Sandwich Generation"

Writing for a specific audience is vital to any publication, and the *Houston Business Journal* conducts extensive research to learn about its readers. While the audience varies from small-business owners and managers to Fortune 500 executives and CEOs, they all have one thing in common—they are an impressive clientele.

The advertisements show that readers' interests run the gamut, from buying a luxury car or finding an exclusive jeweler to searching for the most suitable retirement communities and the best area restaurants.

"Our readers are typically affluent people with a large amount of discre-

Houston Business Journal **staff gather at the paper's eighth-annual golf tournament benefitting Texas Children's Hospital.**

The *Houston Business Journal* publishes 52 issues per year, in addition to the annual *Book of Lists*.

tionary income. They are the Sandwich Generation—putting their kids through school while supporting their senior parents," Beddow says.

More Than Just News

In response to its diverse audience, the journal makes it a priority to provide a variety of information. A feature called Growth Strategies offers lessons learned and helpful articles for emerging companies. The section features columns by experts on everything from being a savvy shopper to shoestring marketing.

In each issue, the newspaper dedicates its Focus section to examining areas such as education and training or banking and finance. The journal's well-known Top 25 list falls in with each issue's Focus section. These lists are then compiled into the company's annual *Book of Lists*.

In addition, the journal staff compiles a number of special publications throughout the year to feature certain industries or areas of interest such as *Philanthropy Magazine* or *Tech.com*. Special publications such as these are produced about eight times a year. Some publications honor businesses at award events, while other sections allow Houston to get an in-depth view of the current issues in an industry. For example, the *Philanthropy Magazine* was released prior to an event that honored six local large and small businesses for their contribution of time, products,

and money to the city.

On the other hand, "Our Public Company Quarterly section lists all the publicly held companies in town," Beddow says. "We had a research group compile a prospectus for our readers. It wasn't an easy task. There's no place to go and click on a button requesting that kind of information. Without this publication, this valuable information wouldn't be available to the Houston communities."

Though the *Houston Business Journal*'s main focus is on business, the diverse needs of its readers and of the greater community continually push the journal in new directions. It offers more than any local daily paper could, and in that way, it has created a unique market segment for itself. Having demonstrated both its capacity for growth and change and its solid journalistic merit, the *Houston Business Journal* proves to be an exemplary media source.

John Beddow serves as publisher of the *Houston Business Journal*.

Houston Community College System

As the largest community college on the Texas Gulf Coast and the third largest in Texas, the Houston Community College System (HCCS) is an academic front-runner in anticipating and responding to future workplace trends, offering a broad range of associate degrees, certificates, and continuing education programs.

Clockwise from top:
At Houston Community College System's (HCCS) Roland Smith Commercial Truck Driving School, students learn the skills needed to land lucrative jobs in one of the nation's fastest growing fields.

In 1999, HCCS opened the John B. Coleman Health Science Center, a state-of-the-art permanent education facility in the world-renowned Texas Medical Center. The Coleman building houses 17 nursing and health-related programs, making HCCS one of the largest providers of health care training in the state.

HCCS boasts some of the best computer labs in the nation, offering instruction in areas such as database software, graphic design, and technical communication. At each of HCCS' five campuses, students and staff have access to the latest PC and Macintosh systems. Training leading to certification by Oracle and Microsoft is also available.

HCCS is committed to meeting the educational needs of its diverse population, and is a model for urban community colleges across the nation. Established in 1971 by the Houston Independent School District to provide postsecondary education, HCCS became autonomous in 1989, and has since expanded its programs to enrich academic learning and prepare the workforce for the 21st century. The system, which boasts five regional colleges, enrolls nearly 55,000 students and has served more than 1 million students since opening its doors in 1971.

HCCS is the largest provider of technical training in Texas, offering top-flight programs designed to meet the needs of the city's business community and its rapidly changing technology. Popular high-tech programs include fiber optics, safety and environmental technology, and biomedical electronics. In addition to technical programs, the college offers academic transfer courses and continuing education, ranging from English as a second language to adult literacy programs, as well as a full range of contract training programs and seminars.

The Workforce Development Unit is a continuously expanding department that has created an industry-driven division for HCCS. In response to industry needs, it recently introduced several new programs, including the Geographic Information Science (GIS) program and the Oracle Training Center. GIS, a computer-based program that combines surveying, remote sensing, and computer science to analyze spatial data and produce specialized maps, is in high demand by oil companies, utilities, municipalities, shipping, transportation, and emergency services.

The Oracle Training Center was developed at the request of Oracle Corporation, one of the world's largest providers of database software, to address the shortage of computer technicians with Oracle backgrounds. In addition, in 2000, the college launched a Microsoft Certified Systems Engineering program, in partnership with IBM, that specializes in the installation and maintenance of computer network systems.

Community Partners

HCCS provides educational services to more than 160 companies, including Lyondell Petrochemical, Southwestern Bell Telephone, NASA, Texaco, Cooper Industries, and Shell Oil. While the college system prepares students for these high-tech careers, other top workforce programs—including paramedic training, construction technology, commercial truck driver training, criminal justice, culinary services, and health sciences—meet the needs of local industries.

In 1999, HCCS became the first community college to build a permanent education facility in the world-renowned Texas Medical Center by opening the John B. Coleman Health Science Center, which offers 17 nursing and health-related programs. Six other new facilities also were built around the city, further enabling the college to offer convenient, high-technology programs to an increasing number of students.

As an integral part of the community, HCCS works to provide quality programs and services that will help to put all Houstonians in the forefront of economic and social development in the 21st century.

Life in Fort Bend County runs the gamut of everything Texan. Business opportunities, a pleasant quality of life, impressive education systems, historic sites, a touch of country, and a can-do spirit all define Fort Bend, one of the fastest-growing counties in the nation. "It's all the Texas you're looking for," says Louis Garvin, CEO of the Fort

Bend Chamber of Commerce. "Everything people admire about Texas comes together here in Fort Bend, making it a great place to live, work, and raise a family."

● The Fort Bend Chamber was founded in 1972, and now provides leadership, networking, and information services to more than 1,650 Fort Bend businesses.

In addition, the chamber serves more than 360,000 residents in several cities, including Sugar Land, Stafford, Missouri City, Meadows Place, Rosenberg, and Richmond, the county seat.

Progress, Texas Style

Fort Bend County is bursting with new development, including Katy Mills and First Colony malls, a 24-screen movie theater, Methodist Health Center, and numerous upscale business parks.

A surge in business and residential development has caused some areas of the county, such as Sugar Land, to triple in size in the last 10 years. Garvin reports that the ratio of Fort Bend residents who work in Houston used to be 65-to-35 in 1985; now, it's closer to 50-50.

To make it easier for those who continue to make the commute, the $120 million expansion of the Southwest Freeway has begun. By 2003, U.S. Highway 59 will have eight lanes with three-lane frontage roads from Houston to just south of State Highway 6.

The area's educational offerings are comprehensive, from exemplary schools in the Fort Bend, Stafford, and Lamar school districts, to higher education opportunities at Houston Community College in Stafford, Wharton County Junior College in Sugar Land, and the University of Houston-Fort Bend. Recently, the University of Houston-Sugar Land broke ground to build its campus on Highway 59 near the Brazos River.

Master-planned communities feature more than 300 acres of lakes, 600 acres of parks, and several country clubs offering more than 250 holes of golf.

A Rich History

Fort Bend is steeped in history, dating back more than 150 years. The Fort Bend Museum in Richmond chronicles the settling of the area. The 500-acre George Ranch Historical Park brings 170 years of Texas ranching to life. Imperial Sugar Company still operates the state's

only cane sugar refinery on the same site where it was built in 1843. Even the chamber is located in a historic site, a refurbished 1927 railroad depot in Sugar Land.

In addition, visitors can explore faraway galaxies at the George Observatory and Fort Bend Challenger Learning Center located at Brazos Bend State Park.

Future plans for Fort Bend call for the addition of a full-service hotel and conference center. And the chamber has launched

a campaign called Fort Bend 2010 and Beyond, which will develop plans for the county's growing infrastructure, making sure Fort Bend continues to deliver everything Texan.

From top:

Fort Bend County is a thriving community of combined values where virtues of small-town living and the sophistication of a global economy come together.

Fort Bend has capitalized on the high quality of life sought after by families looking for the right place to call home with master-planned communities such as Sienna Plantation, First Colony, Cinco Ranch, Greatwood, River Park, and many others.

Historic and adventurous locations offer visitors both relaxing business settings and fun family getaways, making Fort Bend County truly "all the Texas you're looking for."

© PAUL HESTER

CITY IN MOTION

1973

NORTH HARRIS MONTGOMERY
  COMMUNITY COLLEGE DISTRICT

1975

HOUSTON WEST CHAMBER OF COMMERCE

1976

HOUSTON HISPANIC CHAMBER OF COMMERCE

1978

THE ART INSTITUTE OF HOUSTON

1980

PTI, INCORPORATED

1982

BOYAR & MILLER

1984

CLEAR LAKE AREA ECONOMIC
  DEVELOPMENT FOUNDATION

1984

FRONT OFFICE BUSINESS CENTERS

1988

DOUBLETREE HOTEL AT POST OAK

1989

ANDERSEN CONSULTING

1990

WICKLIFF & HALL, PC

1995

DREYER'S GRAND ICE CREAM

1996

BAYKO GIBSON CARNEGIE & HAGAN LLP

North Harris Montgomery Community College District

For more than 25 years, North Harris Montgomery Community College District has not only been meeting the needs of the community by providing a diverse array of educational offerings, but has also been building successful partnerships—partnerships that have taken the district into new arenas both locally and globally. ● "Through our partnerships, we seek to maximize our offerings, becoming a positive force in the intellectual, cultural, and economic success of the north Houston region," says Chancellor John E. Pickelman, Ph.D. The district's board, administration, faculty, and staff have engaged in dozens of

partnerships with the community, public schools, universities, and businesses in Houston and other cities around the world.

The district began in 1973 with 613 students in classrooms provided by the Aldine Independent School District. Today, those numbers have multiplied to an average of 50,000 students enrolled in credit and non-credit courses each year, making North Harris Montgomery the fifth-largest community college district in Texas.

The district provides educational programs for certificates, degrees, training, and retraining at its four college campuses—North Harris College, Kingwood College, Tomball College, and Montgomery College. Working with six Texas universities, the district offers 26 bachelor's degrees and 23 master's degrees through its University Center in The Woodlands.

In conjunction with local high schools, the district offers the Shared Counselor Program, which assists students with college decisions, and the Dual Credit Program, which allows students to take classes and qualify for both high school and college credit. "Our goal is to promote a seamless educational journey, and these partnerships enable that to happen," Pickelman says.

An Active Force in the Community

The district has pursued many economic and workforce development initiatives with chambers of commerce, local businesses, and individuals to promote the economic health of the community, as well as to provide workforce training. The North Houston Economic Development Alliance partners the district with 18 chambers of commerce and economic development organizations that represent 46,000 area businesses. The alliance is a strong force that promotes economic, small business, and workforce development through the sharing of information, resources, expertise, funds, and facilities.

Collaborating with private industry, the district addresses the professional development of full-time and adjunct community college faculty by sponsoring the Center

for Technology and Distance Learning, where teachers are trained in the integration of technology into college courses. "This partnership is one example of the district's commitment to maximizing the use of information technology, interactive systems, Internet applications, and telecommunications in its educational offerings," Pickelman says.

Another partnership, called the Aldine Public School Initiative, provides shared facilities, resources, counselors, and curriculum development to students in pre-K through high school.

The district remains a leader in Tech Prep/School-to-Careers and quality workforce planning. Through TechForce 2000, the district provides leadership to a 13-county area in the use of technology, sharing workforce and labor market information among institutions, business, government, labor, and educators.

The district's state-of-the-art facilities not only provide exciting learning environments for students, but also welcome community events such as chamber meetings, business fests, community arts festivals, and fun runs. "We're proud to have been a positive force in the north Houston region for more than 25 years, and we look forward to another 25 years of success for the region," Pickelman says.

As the fifth-largest community college district in Texas, the North Harris Montgomery Community College District services the academic interests of students throughout the greater Houston area.

The Houston West Chamber of Commerce is positioning itself for the new millennium. By 2010, it is anticipated that Houston's population will be concentrated at Interstate 10 and Highway 6, virtually in the center of Houston West's service area. With such growth on the horizon, the chamber is taking steps to ensure that the rise in population is complemented by steady economic growth in the community. ● "We consider ourselves the voice for business, and we are working to bring in businesses that support the citizens of the West Houston area," says Carolyn Wright, president and CEO of the Houston West Chamber of Commerce, which was established in 1975. The area's boundaries are Highway 290 on the north, the 610 Loop on the east, Highway 59 on the south, and the city of Katy on the west. Within those boundaries are many of Houston's high-technology and energy-related companies.

"We are known as the Energy Corridor of Houston. Many of the city's oil companies have their headquarters right here in West Houston," Wright says. She adds that, of the 73 consulates in the city, the majority are located in the area.

An Attractive Area to Work and Live

West Houston's high quality of life is a key reason for such solid economic growth and high business retention. The area is serviced by five major highway arteries—Beltway 8, Interstate 10, U.S. 59, Highway 290, and Loop 610—and boasts a number of major health care facilities. "From primary care to specialty surgery, residents of West Houston can choose from hundreds of doctors and specialists," Wright says.

With an average annual household income of more than $50,000, West Houston offers just about every type of housing imaginable—from wood-framed bungalows to contemporary designs to stately mansions.

Educational opportunities abound in West Houston, and the area is served by five school districts—Houston ISD, Alief ISD, Cy-Fair ISD, Katy ISD, and Spring Branch ISD—as well as eight private schools.

Shopping and entertainment are never more than a few minutes away. Home to the city's famed Galleria Mall, West Houston offers some of the world's finest shopping opportunities, with a broad assortment of malls and shopping villages. Golf courses, nature trails, and movie complexes also abound in the area.

The Voice for Business

The Houston West Chamber of Commerce considers one of its roles in the community to be a support network for small and medium-sized businesses. In addition to hosting an annual International Expo, where the 73 consuls in Houston advise companies on exporting and importing opportunities, the chamber also provides a number of networking events through monthly meetings and volunteer opportunities on committees.

To accommodate a growing number of home-based businesses in West Houston, the chamber has developed a training center, which provides small seminars geared toward helping home-based businesses, as well as small and medium-sized companies. Says Wright, "We are taking an active role in helping companies in the West Houston area grow their businesses."

The Houston West Chamber of Commerce is working to ensure the success not only of West Houston, but of the entire metropolitan area.

When 15 Hispanic business leaders came together in 1976 to form the Houston Hispanic Chamber of Commerce, they were looking for little more than opportunities to network and promote their businesses. Today, the chamber has not only evolved into one of the largest and fastest-growing chambers in the Houston area, but has also become one of the most innovative and progressive Hispanic chambers in the United States. ● "We are the voice for the Hispanic business owner," says President and CEO Richard R. Torres. "By empowering the Hispanic community to excel in the economic mainstream, we are contributing to the overall growth of the Houston area."

Nationally Recognized Programs

The Houston Hispanic Chamber of Commerce is at the forefront of Hispanic chambers in the country. A member of the U.S. Hispanic Chamber, the Houston organization is a former winner of the Hispanic Chamber of Commerce of the Year Award and has the pleasure of seeing many of its programs emulated nationwide.

Among its recent endeavors is the Hispanic loan program, where the chamber assists business owners in securing bank loans. "Our area businesses need assistance in procuring capital for start-ups and expansions. By acting as a third party between the owner and the bank, we are able to help many businesses secure that necessary capital," Torres says.

Through a partnership with the city's Minority Business Development Center, the chamber also provides technical assistance to minority-owned businesses. The chamber is also the first chamber of commerce to be certified as a third-party intermediary by the Small Business Administration (SBA).

The chamber works with branches of city and county governments to influence public policy and create a positive environment for Hispanic-owned businesses. It has also formed a political action committee, and has taken a more active role in the Hispanic community with the formation of an educational foundation.

Recognizing Outstanding Leadership

In addition to its innovative programs, the chamber also provides traditional networking opportunities for its 1,100 members. The chamber hosts an annual awards ceremony as well, honoring the accomplishments of Hispanic-owned businesses, corporate executives, and corporations that have helped the chamber in furthering its mission.

Houston enjoys the distinction of being the "hometown" of Massey Villarreal—former chairman for the U.S. Hispanic Chamber of Commerce—as well as former chairman Adan Trevino. "We have also become known as a training ground for leaders of Hispanic-owned businesses," Torres says.

The Houston Hispanic Chamber of Commerce has bold projections for the new millennium, and expects to have 10,000 members by 2006. Says Torres, "We are growing together, and we're going in the right direction."

▼ JONATHAN POSTAL/TOWERY PUBLISHING, INC.

The Houston Hispanic Chamber of Commerce has not only evolved into one of the largest and fastest-growing chambers in the Houston area, but has also become one of the most innovative and progressive Hispanic chambers in the country.

With more than 30 years of experience in five states, including a growing office in Houston, Polytech Incorporated—known as PTI, Incorporated—is fast becoming one of the city's leading engineering, architectural, and planning firms. Established in Houston in 1980, PTI offers a comprehensive range of

engineering services, including transportation, mechanical, sanitary, structural, civil, and environmental, as well as design and construction management assistance for a variety of public works projects, land use, and development programs. The company has a diverse client base that includes municipalities, airports, commercial businesses, residential developments, and educational institutions.

Designing the Future

PTI is playing an integral role in improving the city's landscape in the public and private sectors. The company was a member of the Greater Houston Wastewater Program, in which a team of engineers collaborated to develop renovation designs for the city's wastewater collection system. The firm also handled the design and construction management of several highly visible projects around Houston, ranging from the $120 million expansion of the city's East Water Purification Plant to the recent renovation of the downtown headquarters of the Houston Area Urban League.

One of the firm's larger projects involved providing structural engineering services for the design and construction of the $6.8 million, two-story library and computer center at the Palo Alto Community College Learning and Resource Center in San Antonio. PTI also handled the design and construction management of several municipal facilities in the Texas towns of Jasper and Orange.

"This is an exciting period for us. The economy is booming, and there's a lot of major construction taking place on downtown streets, at Bush Intercontinental Airport, and other locations. Some of the best opportunities for business around the country are right here in Houston," says David L. Collins, a civil engineer who heads the Houston firm.

Collins is one of eight principals of PTI, which was originally established in Cleveland, Ohio, in 1969. Today, the company has offices in Cleveland, New York City, Pittsburgh, and Durham, North Carolina, and is one of the nation's most respected minority-owned engineering and architectural consulting firms. Still growing, PTI has 85 employees, including 35 in Houston. "We expect to continue growing and moving into new areas of practice in the 21st century," says Collins.

Giving Back to the Community

In addition to providing superior technical and professional services to a variety of clients, PTI is dedicated to supporting its local community. The company provides pro bono work on an elective basis for organizations in need of engineering services. In 1999, the firm was selected as a finalist for the African-American Business Achievement Pinnacle Award, sponsored by the Houston Citizens Chamber of Commerce and Bank One, for its outstanding business accomplishments and community involvement.

Collins, who is a member of many civic organizations, including the Houston Planning Commission, adds, "Our slogan is, 'We give back to the community,' and that is a large part of who we are as a company."

DAVID BRAY

The Houston office of PTI, Incorporated was established in 1980. PTI principal David L. Collins is pictured here with Houston Mayor Lee P. Brown.

Firmly committed to transforming students' raw talent into functional career skills, the Art Institute of Houston (AIH) has produced some of Houston's top graphic designers, interior designers, and chefs for more than 20 years. As this nationally recognized school enters the new millennium, it plans to continue expanding its curricula and services to meet the rapidly changing demands of Houston's artistic and business communities. The Institute is the school of choice for Houstonians seeking dynamic, exciting careers in the creative and applied arts. Post-secondary career education programs lead students to recognized certificates, diplomas, or Associate of Applied Arts and Associate of Applied Science degrees.

Industry-Driven Programs

With industry-directed curricula, the Institute's primary focus is to cultivate the creativity of students and prepare them for entry-level jobs and career advancement in their chosen fields throughout Houston and the region. In 1998, more than 85 percent of the Institute's graduates (those available for employment) found jobs in their chosen fields within six months of graduation.

AIH programs include computer-aided drafting and design, animation art and design, graphic design, interior design, culinary arts, restaurant and catering management, multimedia, video production, and Web design and development. With credentials in one of these growing fields, graduates can choose from hundreds of rewarding careers, ranging from Web page designer and architectural draftsman to food service manager and animator.

Complementing the range of post-secondary educational opportunities available in Houston, AIH offers courses year-round. The diverse professional faculty brings years of practical work experience—as well as higher education credentials—to the classroom.

Dynamic Student Life

Ideally located on Yorktown, near Houston's uptown Galleria business and retailing district, AIH occupies a six-story building and boasts 77,000 square feet of operating space. In addition to traditional art and lecture classrooms, the Institute features 12 computer labs, a Learning Resource Center, four fully equipped culinary kitchens, audio and video studios, two student lounges, an on-campus restaurant and delicatessen, and an impressive exhibition gallery.

With an entire student body of artistic thinkers, AIH attracts spectators from across Houston to view its monthly gallery exhibits, which include work from local and national artists, as well as students, faculty, and alumni. Located just a few minutes' drive from Houston's art museums and theater district, AIH is situated close to advertising agencies, interior design firms, media outlets, and many of Houston's finest restaurants.

More than 1,600 students, including international students representing more than 25 countries, attend AIH. About 50 percent of the students are from the Greater Houston area. Ranging in age from 18 to 50, the student body is representative of Houston's diverse population.

AIH offers exceptional student services. Convenient, supervised student housing

The Art Institute of Houston prepares its students for exciting careers in a variety of fields, including culinary arts (left) and animation (right).

is available near the campus. Personal, financial, and academic counseling, as well as employment assistance, are also provided. On-campus clubs and organizations, plus planned student activities, make life at AIH fun, educational, and exciting.

National Affiliation

The only institution in Houston dedicated to the applied arts, AIH is a member of the Art Institutes, which includes The Art Institutes in Atlanta, Charlotte, Dallas, Ft. Lauderdale, Los Angeles, Minnesota, Philadelphia, Phoenix, Pittsburgh, Portland, San Francisco, and Seattle; the Colorado Institute of Art in Denver; the Illinois Institute of Art in Chicago; Schaumberg; and the New York Restaurant School.

Among other credentials, AIH is accredited by the Accrediting Commission of Career Schools and Colleges of Technology, and is a candidate for accreditation with the Commission on Colleges of the Southern Association of Colleges and Schools. In addition, the Institute's Culinary Arts program is accredited by the American Culinary Federation.

Regardless of the field of study a student chooses, experienced instructors are there every step of the way to offer guidance and insight.

Like any well-constructed building, a successful business starts with a solid foundation—a set of core values that articulates the company's ideology. For Boyar & Miller, a strong set of values guides the company. "Our core values define how we conduct business," says Chairman Bill Boyar. "We know there are larger firms in our business, but because we're small and well defined, we can move more efficiently, offering our clients a more personal level of service at a very competitive level of sophistication." Established in 1982, this Houston-based law firm's mission is to be a leader in producing value through strategically grounded, results driven service. What started

as a bankruptcy practice by founder Leonard Simon has evolved into two practice groups: the Transaction Group and the Litigation and Bankruptcy Group. Boyar is the firm's chairman, Gary Miller is president and chairman of the Transaction Group, and Michelle Bohreer is chairman of the Litigation and Bankruptcy Group. Leonard Simon remains of counsel. Today, the firm is comprised of 15 attorneys and growing, with a total of about 30 employees, including an executive director, director of marketing and client services, and support staff.

The firm's five core values are each represented by an element of its logo, stylized as a building. The five core values are straightforward: achieving practical business solutions using vision, creativity,

and expertise; highest integrity in all dealings; relentless dedication to service; sustaining an atmosphere of mutual respect, support, and open communication; and balancing commitments to work, family, and community in a way that contributes to professional growth. "It's about being a different kind of law firm, one that maintains a culture where people embrace the core values and feel like they make a difference for each other and for the clients." Miller says.

Adding Value through Personalized Service

The firm serves a myriad of industries. Its clients include small to medium-sized private and public companies and individual entrepreneurs in

such diverse industries as food processing, hospitality, real estate, steel processing, aerospace services, computer technology, e-commerce, venture capital, capital formation, and financial services. Although Boyar & Miller's client base is primarily in Texas, the firm practices on both a national and an international level. "We assist our clients wherever their needs are around the world," Boyar says.

Within the Transaction Group, there are several practice areas: corporate/commercial, entity formation and structuring, real estate, and strategic planning and capital formation. The Litigation and Bankruptcy Group provides commercial litigation, business dispute resolution, bankruptcy, and employment and personnel services.

"We develop strong relationships with our clients. We want to understand the dynamics of their industries. This distinguishes us from the competition and defines who we are and how we operate," Boyar says.

For areas beyond the firm's core competencies, it can tap into a vast network of attorneys around the globe. "This network allows us to provide comprehensive legal services to our clients, while maintaining our focused approach," Boyar says. He cites the example of a global hospitality company the firm represents in North America and western Europe. Boyar travels wherever he is needed for this client. The relationships with various law firms in other areas of the country and in Europe provide a resource pool from which to hire local peripheral firms to meet the needs of the client, such as accounting firms.

(From left) Bill Boyar, firm chairman; Gary Miller, chairman of the Transaction Group

(From left) Bill Manning, legal assistant; Patrick Hayes, transaction associate; Lee Collins, litigation associate; Stephen Johnson, transaction associate

Making a Difference in the Community

In addition to Boyar & Miller's pursuits in the legal arena, the firm is also dedicated to contributing meaningfully in its community. "Our core value of balance means we encourage our employees to grow not only as lawyers and administrators, but also as spouses, parents, and members of the community," Miller explains. "Making family and the community a priority helps to create balance in our lives, and, in turn, makes us better lawyers."

The firm's employees and their families are involved in a variety of organizations throughout the Houston area, including AIDS Foundation of Houston, Camp For All Foundation (of which Miller is president), End Hunger Network, Girl Scouts of America, Houston Food Bank, Houston Livestock Show and Rodeo, Cornerstone Academy-CESIT Program, Kiwanis, Post Oak Montessori School, Rotary Club of Houston, Make-A-Wish Foundation, SEARCH Homeless Project, and Special Olympics.

"We don't just put our money out there. Our people are strongly encouraged to get involved. We have a responsibility to the community," Boyar says. "We take pride in the combination of our contributions to the legal profession and to the community."

As the firm sets its sights on the 21st century, it is committed to additional growth. "We know we're a speedboat on a river of big barges," Boyar says. "But because of our commitment to our core values, as we grow, we will continue to focus on our mission to produce real value for our clients."

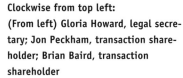

Clockwise from top left:
(From left) Gloria Howard, legal secretary; Jon Peckham, transaction shareholder; Brian Baird, transaction shareholder

(From left) Tim Heinrich, transaction shareholder; Mignon Heizer, executive director and controller; Ginnie Baker, legal secretary

(From left) Michelle Bohreer, Litigation and Bankruptcy Group chairman; Todd Zucker, litigation (of counsel); Trent Rosenthal, bankruptcy shareholder

Clear Lake Area Economic Development Foundation

When the pioneers of NASA's Johnson Space Center first laid eyes on the Clear Lake region, they viewed little more than acres of ranches and rice fields. Today, more than 35 years later, the Clear Lake region has not only become home to the world leader in human space exploration, but has also burgeoned into a well-established eco-nomic center of major industrial and commercial businesses. The 300-square-mile region—which spans south Harris County to north Galveston County and covers parts of 11 cities—is home to a diverse array of industries that include aerospace, aviation, petrochemical, computer software, and biotechnology. Add to that the region's reputation for a high quality of life and its role as an important center for tourism in the Houston area, and the region's slogan comes to life—Clear Lake, Texas: Clearly the Best.

▲ J. PAMELA PHOTOGRAPHY

Partnership in the Community

For 15 years, the area's economic development efforts have been led by the Clear Lake Area Economic Development Foundation. This organization provides the leadership necessary to stimu-late economic development and primary employment in the area. With more than 200 members, the foundation's goal is to develop and utilize responsible, well-planned methods to attract, retain, and expand in-dustry that is compatible with the high quality of life enjoyed by the people in the area.

Through the years, the Johnson Space Center has remained the primary focus and the impetus for new growth in the Clear Lake region. New aerospace support industries have settled near NASA, and the region has evolved into a nucleus of innovation and design. With such leaders of technology centered in one area, the Clear Lake region has attracted a diverse array of other high-tech companies. In addition, leaders in aerospace and aviation have found the region a fruitful area for diversification. "There is a tremendous spirit of enterprise in the area. Many of the top scientists and engineers in the United States are located right here in the Clear Lake Area region," says Jim Reinhartsen, president of the Clear Lake Area Economic Development Foundation.

George W. S. Abbey, center director of the Johnson Space Center, points out the complementary relationship between the area and the aerospace industry: "We are proud of the Johnson Space Center's accomplishments in human space explora-tion. NASA's research and technologies have been applied in many industries and have led to improvments and rich rewards in science, engineering, manufacturing, op-erations, and training activities. We are equally proud to be a part of a great com-munity that has contributed so significantly to the nation's successes in space. As Houston has become a truly international city, the Johnson Space Center has be-come the international focus for human space flight, with an astronaut and engi-neering workforce from nations all over the world."

The Clear Lake region is also home to the Bayport Petrochemical Complex, which houses more than 65 petrochemical com-panies and is one of the largest privately developed industrial facilities in the United States. With a strong international contingent, the complex has attracted businesses from around the globe. In recent years, the Clear Lake region has also become an important resource for petrochemical companies needing off-site office space.

A Center for Tourism

An estimated 1 million people visit the Clear Lake region each year. The area is home to Space Center Houston, the official visitors' center of the Johnson Space Center and the second-largest-attended tourist facility in the state. Designed in cooperation with Walt Disney Imagineering, the $68 million facility offers visitors the experience of space in an en-tertaining and educational way.

Another popular attraction in the area is Clear Lake, a 200-acre natural inlet that has more than 23 marinas and 10,000 boating slips. Clear Lake boasts the third-largest concentration of pleasure boats in the United States and is the boating capital of the state. The lake supports a variety of activities that include waterskiing, jet skiing, parasailing, power boating, and sailing.

The Clear Lake region provides the perfect setting for Armand Bayou Nature

Clockwise from top:
Laura Van Ness serves as vice president of marketing for the Clear Lake Area Economic Development Foundation.

High-technology businesses thrive in the Clear Lake region's business climate.

George W. S. Abbey is center director of the Johnson Space Center.

▲ RICK STYLES

Center, a 1,900-acre nature preserve. And the arts thrive under the guidance of The Arts Alliance Center at Clear Lake, which is the umbrella organization for the Clear Lake Symphony, the Clear Lake Metropolitan Ballet, the Bay Area Symphony League, and the Clear Creek County Theater.

Quality of Life

With housing costs 30 percent below the national average, the living opportunities are diverse. "From premier master-plan communities like South Shore Harbour, which features a golf course and resort complex, to housing that easily accommodates a stable and horses, the Clear Lake region offers affordable living in a community atmosphere for its 185,000 residents," says Thomas E. Brooker, general manager of South Shore Harbour Development Limited.

The region is served by two school districts—Clear Creek Independent School District (ISD) and Friendswood ISD—that are among the top districts in the state. The region is also served by San Jacinto Community College District, College of the Mainland, and University of Houston-Clear Lake, one of only four upper-level universities in the state. "We foster the belief that education is a lifelong process, and we're proud to say that the region can accommodate the educational needs of the community from kindergarten through college," Reinhartsen says.

The Clear Lake region is served by six major health care facilities and is well-equipped to handle virtually any medical need. For those needing specialized care, the region is situated between the Texas Medical Center in Houston and the University of Texas Medical Branch in Galveston. "Some of the top medical research facilities in the United States are only 25 miles away," Reinhartsen says.

"As a destination for burgeoning new industries, new residents, and tourists, the Clear Lake region has attracted people and businesses from around the world," says Laura Van Ness, vice president of the Clear Lake Area Economic Development Foundation. Through continued growth under the leadership of the organization, the area will enjoy its excellent reputation for many years to come.

Through the years, the Johnson Space Center has remained the primary focus and the impetus for new growth in the Clear Lake region. New aerospace support industries have settled near NASA, and the region has evolved into a nucleus of innovation and design.

Another popular attraction in the area is Clear Lake, a 200-acre natural inlet that combines the waters of Clear Creek and Galveston Bay. With more than 23 marinas and 10,000 boating slips, Clear Lake boasts the largest concentration of pleasure boats in the United States and is the boating capital of the state. The lake supports a variety of activities that include waterskiing, jet skiing, parasailing, powerboating, and sailing.

▲ CLIFF MEINHARDT

When Aleta Pippin opened her first executive suite in 1984, her goal was to provide a quality office environment with a support staff that delivered personalized, professional service beyond the client's expectations. Four locations and 15 years later, Front Office Business Centers remains steadfastly loyal to this goal and has emerged as a leader in Houston's executive suite industry. "Any executive suite can provide an office. What sets us apart from the competition is the level of customer support we provide," says Pippin, who co-owns Front Office Business Centers with her husband, E.V. Weaver.

Tailored Support Services

For individuals, entrepreneurs, or large companies opening satellite offices, the suites enable companies or business professionals to establish a presence in Houston without the time and expense of added personnel, furniture, and equipment. Front Office's support staff provides receptionist, secretarial, desktop publishing, and graphic design services,

Front Office Business Centers has four prime locations around town: its Galleria location, which is across the street from the world-famous Galleria Mall, in the heart of Houston's financial district (bottom right); its prestigious One Riverway location, which is a short commute from downtown (not shown); its One Westchase location in West Houston, one of the city's fastest-growing areas (bottom left); and its Phoenix Tower location, just 15 minutes from downtown or the Medical Center (top).

and each suite houses conference rooms and an attractive reception area.

"Every client has different needs," says Karen Hatler, general manager. "While some people need offices in the suites, other clients only require receptionist support and conference room use. We tailor our services to the individual's needs."

Front Office maintains its exemplary customer service level by constantly training and mentoring its staff, as well as by providing top salaries in the industry. "Our employees are our number-one resource. By investing in them, we are working to create a professional and positive environment," Hatler says.

Front Office has named its secretarial staff the First Impressions, and its information processors the Resource Pros. Each group meets monthly for focus sessions and ongoing training. Hatler adds, "We approach our meetings with the question, 'How can we better support our clients?'"

Location, Location, Location

Front Office has four prime locations around town: its Galleria location, which is across the street from the

world-famous Galleria Mall, in the heart of Houston's financial district; its prestigious One Riverway location, which is a short commute from downtown; its One Westchase location in West Houston, one of the city's fastest-growing areas; and its Phoenix Tower location, just 15 minutes from downtown or the Medical Center.

In addition to personalized support services, Front Office works to create a shared community by hosting networking luncheons and meetings. "We have a unique situation, where clients of very different professional backgrounds may be in offices right next to each other. We want to create a sense of connection to each other," Hatler says.

As part of its effort to extend the reach of its services beyond the Houston area, Front Office is a member of the Alliance Business Centers Network, an international organization that markets executive suite services. "If an executive needs temporary access to an office or conference room for day use in Beijing, China, we can easily put our clients in touch with local services," Hatler says.

Front Office is also a member of the Executive Suite Association, a trade organization that meets monthly to discuss changes in technology.

"In order to provide the best in services, we keep on top of changes in the industry," Pippin says. She sees the Houston economy as robust and a fruitful area for growth.

"We don't know what's on the horizon, but we are always open to new opportunities."

Dreyer's Grand Ice Cream—now the largest premium ice cream company in the United States—started out as a small operation in the Oakland Bay Area. In 1928, William Dreyer, who had recently immigrated to this country, began making ice cream in a small shop on Grand Avenue. He partnered with Joseph Edy, who supplied Dreyer with nuts and candies, and sold the hand-packed pints and cones from his candy store and to local restaurants. ● It wasn't long until Dreyer and Edy began experimenting with new combinations of flavorings and added ingredients. In the fall of 1929, the inspiration for the name of their newest creation—chocolate

ice cream with marshmallows and almonds—came from local newspaper headlines. As the stock market crashed, the newspaper proclaimed, "The country is in for a Rocky Road." To sweeten the blow, Dreyer's named this now classic flavor Rocky Road. Many popular new flavors followed, such as toasted almond and mint chip, setting the stage for Dreyer's to become the leader in new product introductions such as light dairy desserts, frozen yogurt, no-sugar-added products, and a host of innovative new flavors. This type of ingenuity has placed Dreyer's as the industry leader, with more than $1.2 billion in annual sales.

While the company remains headquartered in Oakland, Dreyer's has grown to have national distribution through its world class Direct Store Delivery (DSD) system. "By being DSD, we can place the right product on the right shelf at the right time anywhere in the United States," says Houston Plant Manager Scott West. DSD is also a key to maintaining the quality of the product and presenting flavor opportunities for

the consumer. "Our distribution organization allows us to execute many special events such as holiday seasonal flavors, motion picture tie-ins and sports team products."

This distribution network is supported by manufacturing plants in California, Indiana, Utah, and most recently Houston. The Texas Operations Center, as it is called within Dreyer's, opened its doors in the fall of 1995 and now supports more than 300 manufacturing and distribution employees. By producing close to 30 million gallons of ice cream each year, the Texas Operations Center supplies a broad range of products for consumers in Texas, across the Gulf States, and throughout the Southeast. Some of the products manufactured and distributed in Texas include Dreyer's and Edy's branded products, as well as Dreamery, Mars, Starbucks, Godiva, and Healthy Choice ice creams.

West attributes the company's continued success to its attitude that each and every employee can make a difference. "We seek to empower our employees, and

our systems and processes are designed so that our team members have a stake in the company," he says. Dreyer's is also known for its state-of-the-art equipment, as well as for its technical and food science innovation. "We are always looking ahead to what's new on the horizon," West says. "To be first to market, we partner very closely with select equipment and ingredient suppliers to ensure we stay one step ahead of the competition."

The company's close connection to the local community certainly has its advantages for Houston's citizens. Dreyer's not only ensures that grocery store shelves are stocked, but also participates in many charity and benefit events around town. "We do a lot of product donations throughout the year. Many are smaller groups like schools and churches, but we also do some of the larger events like the fund-raiser at the Houston Zoological Gardens," West says.

West adds that the plant expects to continue growing its local business through the addition of new products. "Dreyer's Grand Ice Cream is the leading national ice cream company for many reasons, but mostly due to innovative new products, a quality orientation from the cows all the way to the consumers, and empowered team members who are great at what they do," West says.

▲ BRUCE GLASS

Dreyer's Grand Ice Cream's Texas Operations Center opened in 1995 and now supports more than 300 manufacturing and distribution employees.

DoubleTree Hotel at Post Oak

Strides away from the hustle and bustle of Houston's uptown Galleria area lies a stylistically distinctive, 14-story structure of rusticated pink granite. Home to the DoubleTree Hotel since 1988, the dramatic building, designed by world-famous architect I.M. Pei, projects a sense of permanence and elegance amid the international prestige of the uptown district. An award-winning design, the building's dramatic effect doesn't stop with its outer structure. Beyond the glass-domed porte cochere awaits an inviting lobby that harmonizes gracefully with the bold architecture. ● Custom design rules. Each meeting room creates an experience with its own distinct personality. The Vendome Room features carved oak paneling, taken from a 19th-century French château. Circa-1815-style wallpaper complemented by wood paneling framework dominates the Concord Room. And, the grandest of them all, the Grand Ballroom has been smartly designed to divide off into three separate rooms for functions du jour. French-inspired bands of latticework adorn the ceiling, concealing sprinklers and speakers. Visitors also find swagged silk draperies and Corinthian column capitals. And for the pièce de résistance, the floor is graced by carpeting based on a Louis XVI design.

Sweet Taste of Customized Service

The custom design of the hotel is complemented by DoubleTree's exemplary customized service, provided by a bilingual staff and backed by a 100 percent satisfaction guarantee. "We take pride in ensuring our guests and visitors receive the highest level of service," says Harry Greenblatt, general manager.

Guests are greeted upon arrival with a warm bag of DoubleTree's signature chocolate-chip cookies, baked fresh daily at the hotel. The concierge staff anticipates needs and eagerly fills requests for courier service, transportation services, baby-sitting arrangements, and complimentary shuttle service within a three-mile radius of the hotel. The Business Class floor caters to the executive traveler with upgraded VIP amenities and an office-away-from-the-office business center for services such as faxing and photocopying.

The DoubleTree, a AAA four-diamond hotel owned by Hilton Hotel Corporation, offers 449 spacious guest rooms, including 22 junior suites, 13 one- and two-bedroom suites, and two presidential suites. Each of the elegantly appointed rooms and suites opens onto a balcony presenting views of the uptown Houston area. Rooms are equipped with a card-key system to assure guest-room security, and the hotel offers 24-hour room service.

The junior suites feature a wet bar and refrigerator; an informal living area separated by a wood-paneled armoire, which encases a swivel TV; and a Texas-sized bathroom with a double vanity.

The two presidential suites are custom designed and feature a marble-floored entry, formal and informal living rooms, a dining room, a wet bar, a guest bath, a master bath with Jacuzzi, a separate shower, and two dressing areas with connecting rooms.

Travelers enjoy the amenities of a pool with cabana bar, exercise facilities, and sauna. On the lobby level, the hotel features a full-service men's and ladies' salon, shoe-shine service, a gift and sundries shop, and Capricio Creations, an Italian designer shop for men and women. The hotel also offers dry cleaning and laundry service and valet parking.

A Menu of Delicious Delights

DoubleTree's food and beverage services are orchestrated by chef David Levin. "With David at the helm, guests enjoy the finest of fare," Greenblatt says. The hotel is proud to announce it has added a new kosher kitchen to better accommodate the dining needs of Jewish guests.

For breakfast and lunch, guests dine at

The DoubleTree Hotel at Post Oak, a AAA four-diamond hotel managed by Hilton Hotel Corporation, offers 449 spacious guest rooms, including 22 junior suites, 13 one- and two-bedroom suites, and two presidential suites (left).

DoubleTree's food and beverage services are orchestrated by chef David Levin (right).

For breakfast and lunch, guests dine at the Promenade Restaurant, an American grill offering a menu of favorites in a casual atmosphere.

the Promenade Restaurant, an American grill offering a menu of favorites in a casual atmosphere. For dinner, guests enjoy one of Houston's finest upscale steak restaurants, the Steak & Chophouse on the Boulevard. After dinner, drinks and snacks can be had at the Brittney Bar, a cozy, English-style pub, decorated with wood paneling and French oil lamps.

The DoubleTree is an ideal retreat for daytime business functions. Seminar and luncheon participants enjoy the benefits of state-of-the-art audiovisual equipment housed discreetly in elegant and distinguished conference rooms. The hotel offers a variety of meeting rooms, accommodating cozy gatherings up to formal receptions of more than 1,500 guests. An annual host to the Consular Ball and a setting for many of Houston's high-society weddings, the DoubleTree is a gracious host for distinguished guests and holds true to its commitment to exemplary service.

Loyal to the Houston community, the DoubleTree is an avid supporter of many local organizations. Regular donations are made to the Houston Food Bank and local homeless shelters, and staff and food are provided pro bono for the annual fund drive of the Society for the Prevention of Cruelty to Animals (SPCA), among other functions. The hotel also participates in a corporatewide Christmas program, Grant-A-Wish, where the hotel offers complimentary accommodations to families with loved ones in the hospital. "The Houston area has been so good to us over the years. We welcome the opportunity to give back to the community whenever we can," Greenblatt says.

On the lobby level, the hotel features a full-service men's and ladies' salon, shoe-shine service, a gift and sundries shop, and Capricio Creations, an Italian designer shop for men and women.

Andersen Consulting

Andersen Consulting is not a typical consulting firm. The industrial economy has given way to the electronic economy. The convergence of computing, communication, and content technologies has spawned a new economy with an entirely new set of rules, opportunities, threats, and challenges. "Andersen Consulting is committed to helping clients understand the impact of e-commerce and guiding them through the necessary transformation their companies must make to be successful in e-economy," says Joe W. Forehand, managing partner and CEO. "As a testament to our commitment, we have invested significant resources into research, the creation of thought leadership, and the development of unique resources."

With more than 65,000 people in 48 countries—1,300 in Houston—and revenues of $8.9 billion, Andersen Consulting has the business-savvy professionals to address virtually any client's challenge. Eighty-five of the Fortune Global 100 companies and nearly 75 percent of Fortune's most profitable firms are Andersen Consulting clients.

In the e-world, the firm's clients include more than half of both the Fortune Global 500 and The Industry Standard 100 most important companies of the Internet economy. The firm also serves more than half of the Fortune e50, the companies leading the charge in e-economy. The firm's electronic commerce revenues for 1999 topped $1.5 billion—triple the amount earned in 1998. This dramatic increase is a testament to Andersen Consulting's focus on providing the world's foremost global e-commerce capability for blue-chip firms and start-ups alike.

Shaping the New Economy

Andersen Consulting has built a reputation for redefining the consulting industry. Today, it finds itself once again in the pioneering role as the firm adds new ventures and creates new business models to ensure above-market performance and secure its status as a shaper of e-economy.

Part of this strategy has been the formation of AC Ventures in 1999, a new unit that handles capital investments and expands Andersen Consulting's presence in the e-economy. It will invest up to $1 billion over the next five years to create new electronic businesses.

"In addition to the experience and knowledge we have gained through our more than 140 investments and alliances with dot-com companies, we will be able to leverage Andersen Consulting's scale, global presence, and relationships with established industry leaders throughout the world," Forehand says.

"The insights and experience gained through these ventures will bolster our understanding of the dynamics of the new economy and strengthen our ability to forge new models for doing business on the Internet," he adds.

Once funded, Andersen Consulting's Dot-Com Launch Centres can dramatically reduce the time it takes an e-business to go from start-up, to revenue-producing business, and ultimately to successful initial public offering. The 17 centers are strategically located around the world. Each launch site offers Andersen Consulting's unique ability to provide instant experts, real-time solutions, recognized market credibility, and access to its vast network of the world's leading businesses and venture capital firms.

Steve Ballmer, president and CEO of Microsoft (left), and Joe Forehand, managing partner and CEO of Andersen Consulting (right), announce a bold new partnership, which includes the formation of a jointly owned company called Avanade, an Internet and technology services company.

In addition to funding and launching start-ups, Andersen Consulting is partnering with other pioneers of the Web world to create new solutions. The firm has joined Microsoft Corporation in a groundbreaking strategic alliance, which includes the formation of a jointly owned company called Avanade, an Internet and technology services company.

"E-commerce forces enterprises to move quickly from a business strategy to business model changes, and then to scalable solutions. In this environment, companies of all sizes are looking for the right technology solutions and the right expertise to implement it," Forehand says. "This alliance allows us to leverage the strength of Microsoft Windows 2000 platform and our own ability to deliver strategic business and Internet solutions in bringing value to our clients."

Shaping Houston's Future

Community service and involvement are important components of Andersen Consulting's presence in the Houston marketplace. Since 1989, a wide array of civic, economic development, education, arts, and social service organizations have benefited from Andersen Consulting's commitment to give back to the communities in which it does business.

The philanthropic focus of the Houston office is to strike a balance in the giving of funds and volunteer time delivered through programs dedicated to the education, training, and development of young Houstonians. This focus on youth provides the opportunity for Andersen Consulting people to listen to, diagnose, teach, and transfer knowledge—the basics of client work—and to make a difference in the communities where education, training, and development of youth are most needed. Andersen Consulting is proud to support organizations such as Junior Achievement, Juvenile Diabetes Foundation, Big Brothers and Big Sisters, Anson Jones Elementary in HISD, and Sundown Elementary in Katy.

Many of the firm's partners regularly serve as board directors and chairpersons of charity events. Other community service organizations Andersen Consulting is highly involved in are the United Way, Houston Symphony Society, Society of Performing Arts, Houston Grand Opera, SEARCH, Hobby Center for the Performing Arts, Zoo Friends of Houston, and Volunteer Houston.

Two components that shape Houston's future are philanthropy and community service. Partner Jesse Tutor and his wife Betty (center) were chairs of the Houston Symphony Orchestra Millennium Ball. Co-chairs were Diane Gendel (left) and Mary Ann McKeithan (right).

Employees and their families volunteer with charitable organizations and fundraising events—such as the Houston Children's Festival benefiting Child Advocates—dedicated to the education, training, and development of young Houstonians.

Wickliff & Hall, PC

In today's challenging and mercurial legal arena, one Houston-based firm remains poised for change. Wickliff & Hall, PC has been evolving to meet the needs of the tumultuous legal climate for more than 10 years. ● In 1990, A. Martin Wickliff Jr. and Alton J. Hall Jr., products of several of Houston's premier law firms, established their own firm in an effort to create something completely new to the Houston community: a law firm that embraced changing cultural realities and responded quickly to opportunities on the horizon. ● Today, with specialties in commercial litigation, public law, and labor and employment law,

Wickliff & Hall has grown to 30 lawyers and has expanded its reach with satellite offices in Austin and San Antonio. Commitments to excellence, diversity, and the best traditions of the profession have earned the firm a reputation for excellence.

The Wickliff & Hall Difference

Wickliff & Hall serves clients with interests in Texas and the continental United States. Its distinguished client base includes Fortune 500 companies, public and governmental agencies, institutions, nonprofit and charitable organizations, and smaller, emerging companies.

Its respect and appreciation for clients remains one of the firm's hallmarks. "We consider it an honor that clients choose us from among the many law firms in the community," says Wickliff. "They are trusting us to counsel them in matters that are crucial to their well-being and to the success of their business. We take that to heart."

The firm's dedicated and caring attitude

With specialties in commercial litigation, public law, and labor and employment law, Wickliff & Hall has grown to 30 lawyers and has expanded its reach with satellite offices in Austin and San Antonio. Commitments to excellence, diversity, and the best traditions of the profession have earned the firm a reputation for excellence.

Wickliff & Hall's Houston office serves as a hub for the firm's work with local, regional, and national clients.

is manifested in the personalized level of service it provides. Attorneys are available around the clock. They not only answer telephones themselves when in the office, but also communicate with their clients by E-mail. Satisfaction levels are measured with client feedback, and the firm publishes legal updates and occasional client alerts to keep its clients informed of legal developments.

"We work with clients to ensure all their questions are answered fully, ethically, and honestly," Hall says. "We maintain close and cooperative working relationships with them, including in-house counsel when needed. We want to ensure we understand and meet their expectations, and to keep them informed about strategy and the status of a legal matter."

In the firm's attention to fair practices, lawyers confer about costs, staff involved, and the developments and direction of a case. "We work smart to provide good value to our clients," Wickliff says. The firm staffs cases in the most efficient manner possible, and coordinated teamwork between attorneys and staff controls costs and increases efficiencies.

Services Geared to Client Needs

Wickliff & Hall continues to focus on the specialties of trials and litigation of labor and employment cases, commercial and business law, and public law matters, and boasts an impressive 85 percent win record in its trial of cases. It has extensive experience in both state and federal courts. The firm represents corporate and governmental clients also in arbitration and mediation.

The firm's labor and employment law practice represents management in all labor and employment issues in the private and public sectors, and, in addition to litigation and trials, the section provides consultative and compliance services. In addition, Wickliff & Hall offers its clients proactive advice, which focuses on advance planning and avoiding problems by anticipating change. Because of the frequency of transition in labor and employment law, the firm also offers periodic seminars and training sessions to client management, supervisors, and counsel, in addition to providing a quarterly newsletter to its clients.

The firm's extensive and diverse public law practice involves representation of clients on matters such as public finance, general counsel services, and other concerns important to governmental and quasi-governmental entities. Wickliff & Hall represents clients in both public and private sectors.

Excellence through Diversity

Wickliff & Hall's dedication to excellence has earned it numerous accolades over the years. Many of its attorneys have received recognition from their professional peers and have received honors and awards. In addition, many have held office in local, state, and national legal organizations, and several have been elected to prestigious national organizations reserved for the most outstanding lawyers in the field.

Most notably, Wickliff has served on the State Bar of Texas board of directors, as well as on various committees of the State Bar and the Houston Bar Association. He has also served as former president of the Houston Lawyers Association, and Wickliff and Anthony Sadberry are both members of the American Board of Trial Advocates, an elite group of trial lawyers.

The firm is proud to have earned the valued AV rating from *Martindale-Hubbell*, the national directory of American attorneys. In addition, it has been cited by *The American Lawyer* as one of the country's leading law firms used by American corporations; and every year since 1996, *The Bond Buyer* has included the firm in its list of top 10 bond counsel.

Wickliff & Hall considers diversity to be one of its greatest assets. "We're proud to be made up of many gifted and dedicated professionals who come from diverse ethnic, educational, geographic, and cultural backgrounds," Hall says. "We are not all made from the same mold. The exploration of different viewpoints allows our attorneys to use their abilities in creative ways, bringing a greater sensitivity to our clients' concerns."

Wickliff & Hall remains poised for change as new challenges continue to alter the legal profession. "We are pledged to anticipate changes that will impact our clients, providing every client with the full benefits of the Wickliff & Hall difference," Wickliff says.

When Tom Bayko founded Bayko Gibson Carnegie & Hagan LLP in 1996, he knew Houston was the city where he wanted to practice trial law. A product of White & Case, a prestigious Wall Street law firm, Bayko had already gained a reputation as a talented international litigator in his representation of international oil magnate Aramco (now Saudi Aramco) while at White & Case. ● After a relocation brought him to Houston, Bayko set his sights on establishing a law practice in the Bayou City. "Houston is a great place to practice trial law," Bayko says. "It doesn't matter where you're from. In this town, if you're good, you'll succeed."

And, even after such a short span of time, it's clear Bayko Gibson is gaining on the competition. Since its founding, the firm has charted an impressive number of courtroom wins, putting it on the map both locally and around the globe.

International Expertise

The firm represents more than 1,000 clients in the corporate arena. Among them are such giants as Halliburton Company, Union Pacific Railroad Company, Anadarko Petroleum Corporation, ENi S.p.A. of Rome, Crown Central Petroleum Corporation, Kellogg Brown & Root, Coral Energy, L.P., and Reynolds Metals Company.

The firm practices civil litigation in all state and federal courts and international arbitrations. Its transactional and advisory services include environmental, employment, patents, trademarks, copyrights, technology, computer law, securities, and mergers and acquisitions. One of the firm's most well-known cases involved the successful defense of a $15 billion lawsuit concerning the rights to construct the Peace Pipeline from Turkmenistan through Afghanistan into Pakistan. The case, fought in a Fort Bend County court, caught international attention and fostered articles in *The Wall Street Journal*, *The New York Times*, *The Washington Post*, *The Los Angeles Times*, and *The Houston Business Journal*, among others.

Another successful case, in Aberdeen, Scotland, involved the successful representation of a major oil field product manufacturer in the second-longest trial in the history of Scotland. An offshore drilling rig explosion had resulted in $500 million in damages. Bayko Gibson's client, the main target among 13 defendants, was completely exonerated.

With such an international presence, the firm calls upon a global network of resources for local input. "If we need access to legal counsel in virtually any country, it's right at our fingertips," Bayko says. "We go where we are needed." The firm has plans for satellite offices in other major cities in the United States and possibly London.

Maximizing Efficiency through Technology

With a staff of 25 litigators and 25 support personnel, the firm is run "lean and mean," according to Bayko, who adds that the firm maximizes its efficiency through the appropriate use of technology.

Bayko explains that when he started the firm, he hired a team of software engineers to develop a program that would allow the firm to input, access, and sort through millions of documents in a short amount of time. The brainchild of that effort is PaperChaser, which is making headlines throughout the industry. "We've developed a very effective system for dealing with the huge numbers of documents one sees in complex litigation. With PaperChaser, I can sit in the courtroom, sort through millions of documents, and call up what I need—all in a matter of a few seconds. That's a key competitive advantage," Bayko says.

In addition to its use of PaperChaser, the firm updates office technology regularly and makes use of electronic mail to

"We've developed a very effective software program for dealing with the huge number of documents one sees in complex litigation," says Tom Bayko, founder of Bayko Gibson Carnegie & Hagan LLP. In court, Bayko uses his laptop to find—within a few seconds—any item of information contained in the thousands of documents on the shelves next to him.

Some of the talented individuals who have helped Bayko make his firm a success include (seated, from left) Michael Gibson, Michael Ford, (standing, from left) Jack Carnegie, Linda Schoonmaker, Bob Leidich, and Martin Detloff.

improve efficiency. "We will do whatever is needed to make sure we remain as efficient and effective as possible. Technology allows us to maximize our firepower," Bayko says.

Dedication to the Industry and the Community

Another competitive advantage is the firm's highly talented team of attorneys. "We've been lucky to attract such a talented group of people that works tirelessly and with such an exhaustive

dedication. That makes the difference," Bayko says.

The firm also stays active in the community arena, giving of its employees and support to organizations such as the Fort Bend Chamber of Commerce, Houston Bar Foundation, University of Texas Law School Foundation, American Red Cross, Crown of Texas Hospice, American Heart Association, YMCA Partnership for Youth, Fort Bend County Women's Shelter, Easter Seals of Houston, Greater Houston Part-

nership, and the Literacy Council of Fort Bend County. "We're fortunate to be operating in such a great city, and we like to give back whenever we can," Bayko says.

Looking to the future, Bayko plans for continued growth, maneuvering the firm into the fast lane of trial litigation and providing clients with an alternative to the bigger firms in Houston. "We're lean and mean, we work tirelessly for our clients, and we're dedicated to perfection," Bayko says. "You can't beat that."

Since its founding, Bayko Gibson has charted an impressive number of courtroom wins, putting the firm on the map locally and around the globe. Here, Bayko and Carnegie discuss a recent victory.

Towery Publishing, Inc.

Beginning as a small publisher of local newspapers in the 1930s, Towery Publishing, Inc. today produces a wide range of community-oriented materials, including books (Urban Tapestry Series), business directories, magazines, and Internet publications. Building on its long heritage of excellence, the company has become global in scope, with cities from San Diego to Sydney represented by Towery products. In all its endeavors, this Memphis-based company strives to be synonymous with service, utility, and quality.

A Diversity of Community-Based Products

Over the years, Towery has become the largest producer of published materials for North American chambers of commerce. From membership directories that enhance business-to-business communication to visitor and relocation guides tailored to reflect the unique qualities of the communities they cover, the company's chamber-oriented materials offer comprehensive information on dozens of topics, including housing, education, leisure activities, health care, and local government.

In 1998, the company acquired Cincinnati-based Target Marketing, an established provider of detailed city street maps to more than 200 chambers of commerce throughout the United States and Canada. Now a division of Towery, Target offers full-color maps that include local landmarks and points of interest, such as recreational parks, shopping centers, golf courses, schools, industrial parks, city and county limits, subdivision names, public buildings, and even block numbers on most streets.

In 1990, Towery launched the Urban Tapestry Series, an award-winning collection of oversized, hardbound photojournals detailing the people, history, culture, environment, and commerce of various metropolitan areas. These coffee-table books highlight a community through three basic elements: an introductory essay by a noted local individual, an exquisite collection of four-color photographs, and profiles of the companies and organizations that animate the area's business life.

To date, more than 80 Urban Tapestry Series editions have been published in cities around the world, from New York to Vancouver to Sydney. Authors of the books' introductory essays include former U.S. President Gerald Ford (Grand Rapids), former Alberta Premier Peter Lougheed (Calgary), CBS anchor Dan Rather (Austin), ABC anchor Hugh Downs (Phoenix), best-selling mystery author Robert B. Parker (Boston), American Movie Classics host Nick Clooney (Cincinnati), Senator Richard Lugar (Indianapolis), and Challenger Center founder June Scobee Rodgers (Chattanooga).

To maintain hands-on quality in all of its periodicals and books, Towery has long used the latest production methods available. The company was the first production environment in the United States to combine desktop publishing with color separations and image scanning to produce finished film suitable for burning plates for four-color printing. Today, Towery relies on state-of-the-art digital prepress services to produce more than 8,000 pages each year, containing well over 30,000 high-quality color images.

An Internet Pioneer

By combining its long-standing expertise in community-oriented published materials with advanced production capabilities, a global sales force, and extensive data management capabilities, Towery has emerged as a significant provider of Internet-based city information. In keeping with its overall focus on community resources, the company's Internet efforts represent a natural step in the evolution of the business.

The primary product lines within the Internet division are the introCity™ sites.

STEVE DAVIS

Towery Publishing President and CEO J. Robert Towery has expanded the business his parents started in the 1930s to include a growing array of traditional and electronic published materials, as well as Internet and multimedia services, which are marketed locally, nationally, and internationally.

▲ JOHNOTHAN POSTAL

Towery's introCity sites introduce newcomers, visitors, and longtime residents to every facet of a particular community, while simultaneously placing the local chamber of commerce at the forefront of the city's Internet activity. The sites include newcomer information, calendars, photos, citywide business listings with everything from nightlife to shopping to family fun, and on-line maps pinpointing the exact location of businesses, schools, attractions, and much more.

business they had founded nearly four decades earlier. Soon thereafter, he expanded the scope of the company's published materials to include *Memphis* magazine and other successful regional and national publications. In 1985, after selling its locally focused assets, Towery began the trajectory on which it continues today, creating community-oriented materials that are often produced in conjunction with chambers of commerce and other business organizations.

Despite the decades of change, Towery himself follows a long-standing family philosophy of unmatched service and unflinching quality. That approach extends throughout the entire organization, including more than 120 employees at the Memphis headquarters, another 80 located in Northern Kentucky outside Cincinnati, and more than 40 sales, marketing, and editorial staff traveling to and working in a growing list of client cities. All of Towery's products, and more information about the company, are featured on the Internet at www.towery.com.

In summing up his company's steady growth, Towery restates the essential formula that has driven the business since its first pages were published: "The creative energies of our staff drive us toward innovation and invention. Our people make the highest possible demands on themselves, so I know that our future is secure if the ingredients for success remain a focus on service and quality."

Decades of Publishing Expertise

In 1972, current President and CEO J. Robert Towery succeeded his parents in managing the printing and publishing

Towery Publishing was the first producton environment in the United States to combine desktop publishing with color separations and image scanning, to produce finished film suitable for burning plates for four-color printing. Today, the company's state-of-the-art network of Macintosh and Windows workstations allows it to produce more than 8,000 pages each year, containing more than 30,000 high-quality color images.

The Towery family's publishing roots can be traced to 1935, when R.W. Towery (far left) began producing a series of community histories in Tennessee, Mississippi, and Texas. Throughout the company's history, the founding family has consistently exhibited a commitment to clarity, precision, innovation, and vision.

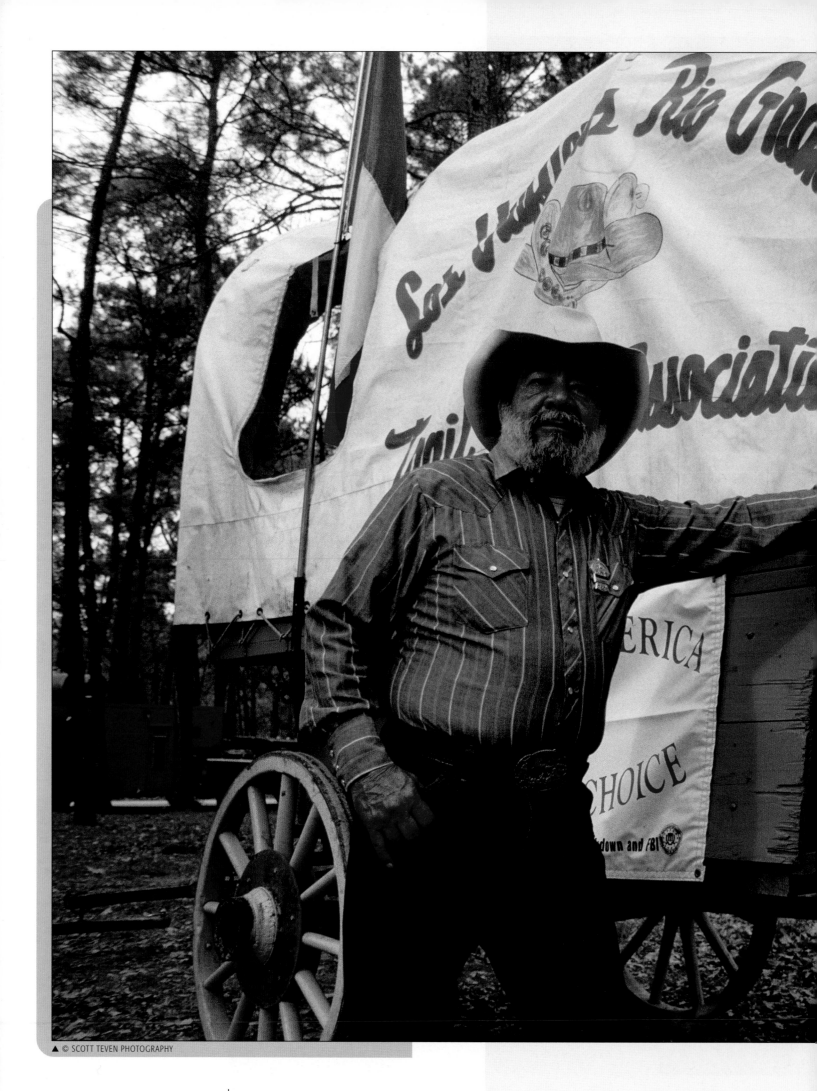

▲ © SCOTT TEVEN PHOTOGRAPHY

LIBRARY OF CONGRESS CATALOGING-IN-PUBLICATION DATA

Connally, Nellie, 1919-

   Houston : city in motion / by Nellie Connally ; art direction by Enrique Espinosa.

      p. cm. – (Urban tapestry series)

   Includes index.

    ISBN 1-881096-81-5 (alk. paper)

    1. Houston (Tex.)–Civilization. 2. Houston (Tex.)–Pictorial works. 3. Houston
(Tex.)–Economic conditions. 4. Business enterprises–Texas–Houston. I. Title II.
Series.

F394.H85 C66 2000

976.4'1411–dc21

00-047666

Printed in China

PUBLISHER: J. Robert Towery EXECUTIVE PUBLISHER: Jenny McDowell NATIONAL
SALES MANAGER: Stephen Hung MARKETING DIRECTOR: Carol Culpepper
PROJECT DIRECTORS: Carolyn Delmar, Henry Hintermeister EXECUTIVE EDITOR:
David B. Dawson MANAGING EDITOR: Lynn Conlee SENIOR EDITORS: Carlisle
Hacker, Brian L. Johnston EDITORS: Jay Adkins, Rebecca E. Farabough, Ginny Reeves,
Sabrina Schroeder EDITOR/CAPTION WRITER: Stephen M. Deusner COPY EDITOR:
Danna M. Greenfield PROFILE WRITERS: Torma Communications CREATIVE
DIRECTOR: Brian Groppe PHOTOGRAPHY EDITOR: Jonathan Postal PHOTOGRAPHIC
CONSULTANT: Maria Moss PROFILE DESIGNERS: Rebekah Barnhardt, Laurie Beck,
Glen Marshall PRODUCTION MANAGER: Brenda Pattat PHOTOGRAPHY COORDI-
NATOR: Robin Lankford PRODUCTION ASSISTANTS: Robert Barnett, Loretta Lane
DIGITAL COLOR SUPERVISOR: Darin Ipema DIGITAL COLOR TECHNICIANS: Eric
Friedl, Brent Salazar COLOR SCANNING TECHNICIANS: Brad Long, Mark Svetz
PRODUCTION RESOURCES MANAGER: Dave Dunlap Jr. PRINT COORDINATOR:
Beverly Timmons

COPYRIGHT © 2000 BY TOWERY PUBLISHING, INC.

ALL RIGHTS RESERVED. NO PART OF THIS WORK MAY BE REPRODUCED OR COPIED IN ANY
FORM OR BY ANY MEANS, EXCEPT FOR BRIEF EXCERPTS IN CONJUNCTION WITH BOOK REVIEWS,
WITHOUT PRIOR WRITTEN PERMISSION OF THE PUBLISHER.

Towery Publishing, Inc.

The Towery Building

1835 Union Avenue

Memphis, TN 38104

www.towery.com

Originally headquartered in London, **Allsport** has expanded to include offices in New York and Los Angeles. Its pictures have appeared in every major publication in the world, and the best of its portfolio has been displayed at elite photographic exhibitions at the Royal Photographic Society and the Olympic Museum in Lausanne.

With an emphasis on special effects photography, **Pat Buron** has been working in the Houston area for more than 20 years. Originally from St. Paul, he attended Houston Community College and is self-employed.

For more than 20 years, **Barry Champagne** has enjoyed photographing Houston, as well as its business, technology, and people. He owns Barry Champagne Photography, Inc. and specializes in architecture, corporate/industrial, and editorial photography.

John Elk III produces travel and location stock photography and has amassed some 250,000 images of North and Central America, Europe, Asia, and Africa. Elk has lived and worked in the Bay Area for 25 years. His clientele includes Hearst Publications, Houghton Mifflin Company, the McGraw-Hill companies, National Geographic Society, Pace Communications, Simon & Schuster, and Macmillan.

Originally from Texas, **Bruce Glass** has lived and worked in the Houston area for 25 years. Bruce Glass Photography specializes in advertising, corporate, industrial, and architectural photography.

Having produced cover photographs for several Houston magazines, **Walter Jiminez** has been published nationally as well as internationally. He operates Walter Jiminez Photography in Houston, and specializes in food, location, industrial, corporate, and stock photography.

Mark Miller and his wife, **Jennifer**, are owners of Mark & Jennifer Miller Photos. Published in *Field & Stream, Country Journal, Outdoor Life,* and *Backpacker,* among others, their work specializes in nature, wildlife, and national parks photography.

Originally from Ohio, **Deron Neblett** attended Rice University, where he studied biology and art history. He specializes in editorial and commercial portraits, and currently operates Deron Neblett Photography.

A lifelong Houston resident, **Bil Olive** has received awards from Out There Advertising and Coldwell Banker. He began his career as a Navy combat photographer and today owns Bil Olive Photography, where he specializes in architectural photography and studio concepts.

Jim Olive, a native of the Houston area, has been published in several local magazines, as well as in national and international publications, and his clients include the *Houston Chronicle,* Greater Houston Partnership, Continental Airlines, and *Tide* magazine, among others. He operates Jim Olive Photography and specializes in corporate, industrial, environmental, and medical photography.

Judi Parks has had her work collected by numerous museums and public collections in the United States and Europe. Her documentary series, *Home Sweet Home: Caring for America's Elderly,* was recently honored with the *Communication Arts-Design Annual* 1999 Award of Excellence for an unpublished series.

Photophile, established in San Diego in 1967, is owned and operated by Nancy Likins-Masten. An internationally known stock photography agency, the company houses more than 1 million color images and

represents more than 90 contributing local and international photographers. Subjects include extensive coverage of the West Coast, business/industry, people/lifestyles, health/medicine, travel, scenics, wildlife, and adventure sports, plus 200 additional categories.

A graduate of Indiana University, **Carl Purcell** is the past director of photography for the Peace Corps and a former employee of the Agency for International Development in the State Department. Residing in Alexandria, Virginia, he and his wife, Ann, work together as the Purcell Team and photograph internationally for such publications as *National Geographic, U.S. News & World Report,* and others.

Janice Rubin specializes in photographing people, family, and educational subjects. Her work has been featured by such companies as Compaq and Exxon Mobil, and has appeared in such publications as *Business Week, Fortune,* and *Smithsonian.* Originally from Fort Worth, she attended Rice University and has lived in the Houston area for more than 25 years.

Specializing in travel photography, **Pam Smedley** works with her husband, David, at David Smedley Photography. Her publications include travel guides and calendars from Delaware and Pennsylvania, and she is one of the official photographers for the State of Delaware Parks and Recreation.

As a Houston native, **Ray Soto** studied photography in Atlanta and began his career producing corporate industrial images. He currently owns a freelance photography studio and services major energy corporations, shipping companies, and advertising agencies.

Since earning his degree in fine arts, **Scott Teven** has photographed Houston for more than 15 years. His work has been purchased for corporate art collections, and he also receives commissions for corporate photo assignments.

Ray Viator has had more than 20 years of experience working with local business leaders, and his work has been featured in several Houston publications and directories. In addition, he has won photography and writing awards in numerous regional competitions.

Please contact Towery Publishing, Inc. for additional information on photographers with images in *Houston: City in Motion.*

▲ © JUDI PARKS

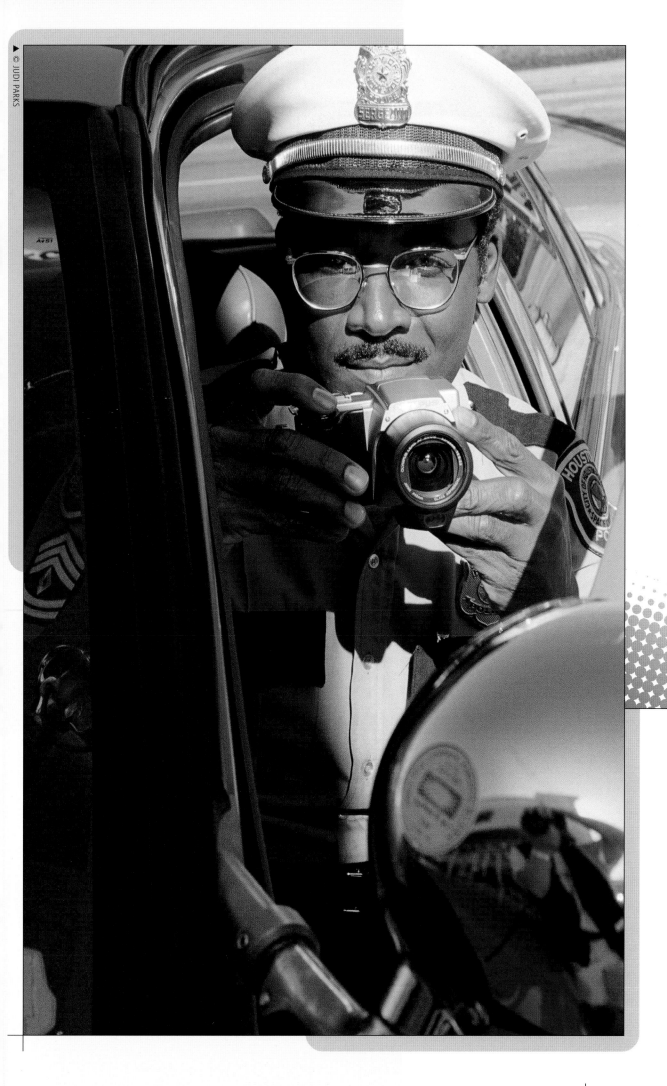

▲ © JUDI PARKS

© RAY VIATOR

CITY IN MOTION

HOUSTON

© JIM OLIVE / STOCKYARD PHOTOS